Souther [African]

Mammals
made simple

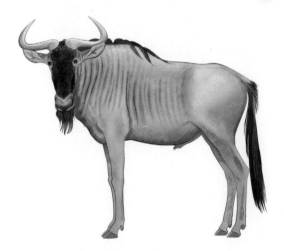

Doug Newman
Gordon King

To Clem Haagner whose mammal recordings have been a constant inspiration. **Doug Newman**

To Sarah, Joan, Andrew, Anthony and Ian King for nurturing my love of nature. **Gordon King**

PHOTOGRAPHERS' ABBREVIATIONS

The authors would like to acknowledge Neil Gray and Gerrie Horn for kindly allowing us to use some of their images free of charge.

(FLPA – Frank Lane Picture Agency; IOA – Images of Africa; NHPA / Photoshot – Natural History Photographic Agency; WC – Wikimedia Commons)
All Wikimedia commons images are distributed under the creative commons licence.

AB – Anthony Bannister
AF – Albert Froneman
AM – Anneli Moeller
AR – Adam Riley
AVZ – Ariadne von Zandbergen
BSTH – BS Turner Hof
CMS – Chris and Mathilde Stuart
CB – C Burnett
CP – Calips
CS – Charles J Sharp
CW – Canis Wolfbane
D - Dori
DG and ER – D Gordon and
  E Robertson
DN – Doug Newman
DP – Devon Pike
F – Fologorando
GH – Gerrie Horn
GK – Gordon King
GMS, FWS – GM Stolz, US Fish
  and Wildlife Service

HH – Hans Hillewaert
HS – Hans Stieglitz
HZ – Harald Zimmer
J – Jeppestown
JD – JagDragon
JG – Joanne Goldby
JR – John Richfield
KF – Karen Fick
LB – Professor Lee Burger
LBR – The Lilac Breasted Roller
LTS – Ltshears
LVH – Lanz von Horsten
LZ – Leo Za1
MBa – Matej Batha
MBu – Marcel Burkhard
MH – Martin Harvey
MP – MichaelPhilipr
MR – Masteraah
ND – Nigel Dennis
NG – Neil Gray
OL – Olivia Lejade

P – Patinowik
PBK – PanBK
PM – Paul Maritz
PP – Phil Perry
RdlH – Roger de la Harpe
RH – Roland Hunziker
S – Sonelle
S and J – Sara and Joachin
SHJ – Shah Jahan
SJ – Steve Jurveston
SK – Sarah King
TC – Tony Camacho
TR – Ton Rulkens
WB – Winfried Beunken
WT – Warwick Tarboton
YE – Yossi Eshbol
YK – Yathin S Krishnappa

Published in 2013 by Struik Nature
an imprint of Random House Struik (Pty) Ltd
Company Reg. No. 1966/003153/07
Wembley Square, First Floor, Solan Road, Gardens,
Cape Town, 8001, South Africa
PO Box 1144, Cape Town, 8000, South Africa
www.randomstruik.co.za

PUBLISHER: Pippa Parker
MANAGING EDITOR: Helen de Villiers
EDITORS: Emily Bowles, Lisa Delaney
DESIGN DIRECTOR: Janice Evans
DESIGN TEAM: Neil Bester, Gillian Black
ILLUSTRATOR: Sally MacLarty
PROOFREADER: Thea Grobbelaar

Maps reproduced from *Smithers' Mammals of Southern Africa: A Field Guide* (2012), Struik Nature, by kind permission of Peter Apps

Reproduction by Hirt and Carter Cape (Pty) Ltd
Printed and bound by Craft Print International Ltd, Singapore

1 2 3 4 5 6 7 8 9 10

ISBN 978 1 92057 238 9

Contents

Introduction

Although some southern African mammals are distinctive, many have features in common with other mammals and are more challenging to tell apart, especially when seen from a distance. This book is designed not as a standard field guide, but rather as a detailed visual guide that simplifies the task of identifying mammals. To distinguish a given species, simply select the appropriate group from each of three sections of the book, which progressively narrow down the field. The sections:

- categorise mammals into broad **'family' groups** on the basis of shared distinguishing features, rather than on their formal taxonomic relationships,
- then, break these 'families' down into **visual groups**, and
- finally, present **species accounts** for each visual group, giving up to three colour-coded key pointers. A successful identification depends on matching one feature in red type or three features in orange type within the visual group.

You must go through all three steps to arrive at the **combination** of family, visual group and key pointers that identifies a particular mammal to species level. So, for example, refer to p.35, which features a female suni:

The three orange pointers highlight 'tiny size', 'hindquarters lack speckling or streaks' and 'reddish-brown hindquarters'. Individually, these characteristics are not helpful for identifying the species. However, if you start at the front of the book and first select the correct **family** (p.10) and then the correct **visual group** within that family (p.21), you will arrive at the suni female (p.35). At this point, the cumulative pointers for this species are:

FAMILY:	✔ hooved feet
	✔ long thin legs
	✔ bare furless horns (if any)
	✔ build is not horse-like
VISUAL GROUP: (BLUE)	✔ no horns
	✔ white belly
	✔ small size
SPECIES KEY POINTERS: (ORANGE/RED)	✔ tiny size
	✔ hindquarters lack speckling or streaks
	✔ reddish-brown hindquarters

For more detailed guidance, see HOW TO USE THIS BOOK, p.7.

The mammals featured here are those that are commonly seen in game reserves and those that are difficult to identify. Species that are very seldom encountered or simply too challenging to identify visually have been omitted. Some rodent and bat species can only be identified by a close inspection of the teeth or skull, and these species are also considered beyond the scope of this book.

Physical characteristics like body size and colour are the most important attributes to take into account when identifying a mammal, but range, habitat and behaviour can also be helpful. When watching mammals, consider the following:

Relative size

In the context of this book, **size is used only to separate species within a particular visual group** and not to separate mammals as a whole. For example, a key pointer for the black-footed cat is 'tiny size', which refers to its size relative to other members of the cats visual group.The blue duiker also has the key pointer 'tiny size', despite being substantially bigger than the black-footed cat, as it, too, is relatively far smaller than the other members of its visual group.

When judging the size of an unfamiliar species, page through the visual group to which you think your example belongs, considering the relative body weights and shoulder heights or nose-to-tail lengths of other species in that group, and then take an educated guess. Gauging size is often easiest when you are already familiar with one or two of the species in the group.

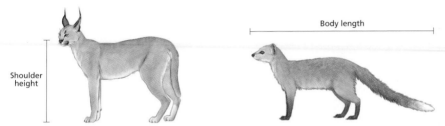

Shoulder height

Body length

Depending on the species, the size measurement given is either height from ground to shoulder, or the length from nose to tail tip.

Colour and markings

Individual colouring and patterns may vary slightly, even within a species. Prevailing light conditions also affect how we perceive an animal's colour and markings. For these reasons, it is important to view the illustrations provided as references rather than perfect reproductions. However, the visual pointers will draw your attention to key features in each illustration. Taking a series of photos from different angles can help you to identify a species later.

The illustrations aim to represent the true colour of each animal, but be aware that colour varies depending on light conditions. For example, the photograph on the far right was taken in the early morning, when the blesbok's coat looks redder than it does in full daylight.

Habits

In some instances, behaviour can help you to identify an animal. A brief description of habits is provided with each species. For example, genets and mongooses are similar in shape, but the former are nocturnal, while the latter are diurnal. Another example is that of black and white rhinos, which feed quite differently. The social behaviour of various antelope can help you to narrow down the options, depending on whether the species is solitary or gathers in much larger groups.

The gemsbok is an example of an antelope that tends to be solitary.

Range and habitat

It is helpful to take into account the range map and usual habitat of a species, as this can considerably narrow down the field of possibilities to choose from. In addition, consulting a species list for the reserve or protected area in which you are spotting mammals can be invaluable.

Bear in mind, though, that some species may occur outside of their traditional ranges or usual habitat. This may be the result of natural disasters, opportunism or human activities, including species management programmes. Smaller mammals, including antelope, cats, dogs, primates and rodents, are easily able to cross reserve boundaries, so you could also be observing a species not previously documented in a given reserve.

> Remember to keep your distance and never interfere with wild animals. Some species quickly become aggressive and dangerous, particularly if they perceive you as a threat to their young.

Rhinos can become aggressive and are best observed from a distance, in the company of experienced rangers.

Each species featured in this book is assigned to one of 14 distinct 'family' groups. As already mentioned, within the context of this book 'family' refers simply to a group of animals that share some broad features and is not to be confused with taxonomic families. In some cases these 'families' are further subdivided into visual groups, the members of which share quite specific physical features.

There are **three** basic steps to identifying your mystery mammal:

STEP ONE: SEPARATING FAMILIES

To decide which of the 14 family groups you are dealing with, refer to pp.9–14, study the illustrations and family features highlighted by the pointers and read the accompanying text. Once you have found the family group to which your mammal belongs, continue to the relevant page as indicated.

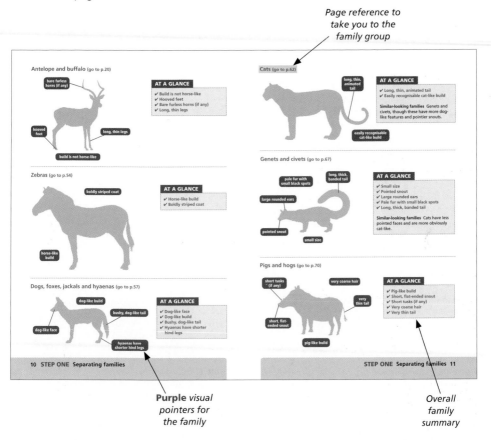

Page reference to take you to the family group

Purple visual pointers for the family

Overall family summary

STEP TWO: SEPARATING THE VISUAL GROUPS

Read the general introduction to the family group, paying particular attention to the features summarised under 'LOOK FOR'. Then study the silhouettes that follow, which present typical or representative species within each visual group.When you have identified the visual group that represents your mammal, follow the page reference and turn to where the species accounts for that visual group start. If there is only a single visual group for that family, then proceed straight to the species accounts.

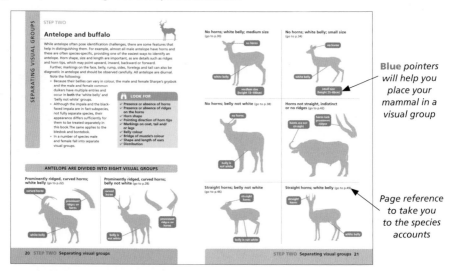

Blue *pointers will help you place your mammal in a visual group*

Page reference to take you to the species accounts

STEP THREE: IDENTIFYING SPECIES

Check each species within the visual group. Pointers on each illustration show the features that separate a particular species from all others **within the same visual group**. Characteristic features are repeated in the 'AT A GLANCE' box at the bottom of the page. This box summarises the *visual* clues and other criteria (for example, distribution) relevant to the identification of that species. Similar-looking species are also listed here.

A successful identification relies on matching all three features in orange **type or one feature in** red **within the visual group.**

In instances where a red feature is given in addition to three orange features, it may be considered as an alternative matching characteristic.

Orange and red diagnostic pointers are applicable for this species only within its blue visual group

'AT A GLANCE' delivers all important information in one place

Additional notes to alert you to possible ID pitfalls

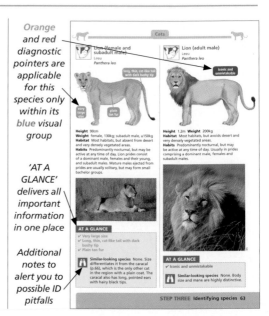

STEP ONE

This step depends on careful scrutiny of the physical appearance of the mammal you wish to identify. Distinctive features are not always strikingly obvious. Among antelope, for instance, one needs to look out for what may be quite subtle tail markings, known as *kleg*. Also take note of the animal's habits and the surrounding habitat, as this may be helpful.

Listed below are the family groups (as understood in the context of this book). Carefully study the characteristic features of each in order to determine the best fit for your mammal. It is important to look at all of the characteristics in the AT A GLANCE box, matching as many as possible to your mammal. This will reduce the margin for error and help you to pinpoint the appropriate family group.

Once you have chosen the family group, proceed to STEP TWO (visual groups) and gradually narrow your choice further.

Water holes, where diverse species gather, are excellent places to observe the differences between various animal families.

Distinctive mammals (go to p.15)
African elephant, hippopotamus, giraffe, porcupine, southern African hedgehog, aardvark, ground pangolin and rhinos. The mammals included in this group are unmistakable and are unlikely to be confused with any others in the region.

AT A GLANCE

Species within this group are all very easy to identify, and share few characteristics. Their distinctive features are very well known.

Antelope and buffalo (go to p.20)

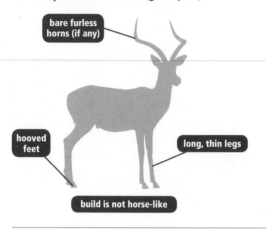

bare furless horns (if any)

hooved feet

long, thin legs

build is not horse-like

AT A GLANCE

✔ Build is not horse-like
✔ Hooved feet
✔ Bare furless horns (if any)
✔ Long, thin legs

Zebras (go to p.54)

boldly striped coat

horse-like build

AT A GLANCE

✔ Horse-like build
✔ Boldly striped coat

Dogs, foxes, jackals and hyaenas (go to p.57)

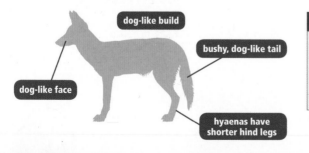

dog-like build

bushy, dog-like tail

dog-like face

hyaenas have shorter hind legs

AT A GLANCE

✔ Dog-like face
✔ Dog-like build
✔ Bushy, dog-like tail
✔ Hyaenas have shorter hind legs

Cats (go to p.62)

long, thin, animated tail

easily recognisable cat-like build

AT A GLANCE

✔ Long, thin, animated tail
✔ Easily recognisable cat-like build

Similar-looking families Genets and civets, though these have more dog-like features and pointier snouts.

Genets and civets (go to p.67)

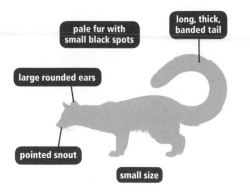

pale fur with small black spots

long, thick, banded tail

large rounded ears

pointed snout

small size

AT A GLANCE

✔ Small size
✔ Pointed snout
✔ Large rounded ears
✔ Pale fur with small black spots
✔ Long, thick, banded tail

Similar-looking families Cats have less pointed faces and are more obviously cat-like.

Pigs and hogs (go to p.70)

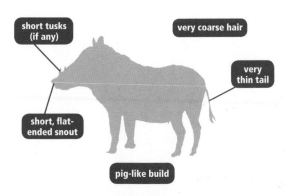

short tusks (if any)

very coarse hair

very thin tail

short, flat-ended snout

pig-like build

AT A GLANCE

✔ Pig-like build
✔ Short, flat-ended snout
✔ Short tusks (if any)
✔ Very coarse hair
✔ Very thin tail

Dassies (hyraxes) (go to p.72)

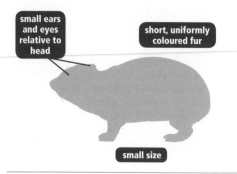

small ears and eyes relative to head

short, uniformly coloured fur

small size

AT A GLANCE

✔ Small size
✔ Small ears and eyes relative to head
✔ Short, uniformly coloured fur

Rabbits and hares (go to p.75)

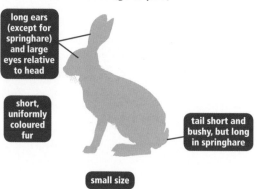

long ears (except for springhare) and large eyes relative to head

short, uniformly coloured fur

tail short and bushy, but long in springhare

small size

AT A GLANCE

✔ Small size
✔ Short, uniformly coloured fur
✔ Long ears (except for springhare) and large eyes relative to head
✔ Tail short and bushy, but long in springhare

Squirrels (go to p.80)

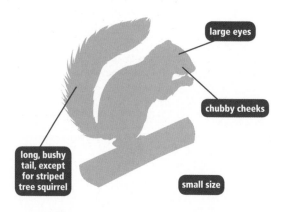

large eyes

chubby cheeks

long, bushy tail, except for striped tree squirrel

small size

AT A GLANCE

✔ Small size
✔ Long, bushy tail, except for striped tree squirrel
✔ Large eyes
✔ Chubby cheeks

Mongooses and suricate (go to p.84)

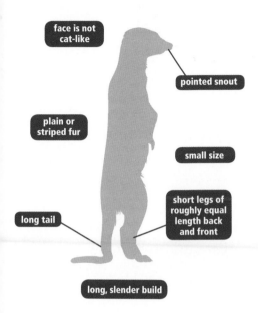

face is not cat-like

pointed snout

plain or striped fur

small size

short legs of roughly equal length back and front

long tail

long, slender build

AT A GLANCE

✔ Long, slender build
✔ Long tail
✔ Plain or striped fur
✔ Face is not cat-like
✔ Pointed snout
✔ Small size
✔ Short legs of roughly equal length back and front

Similar-looking families Behaviourally, a water mongoose may resemble an otter, particularly when seen in the water, but otters have shorter, smoother coats and rounder faces. Mongooses have a similar body shape to striped weasels, but lack the striking black-and-white coat.

Otters (go to p.91)

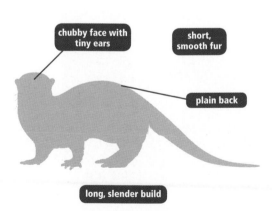

chubby face with tiny ears

short, smooth fur

plain back

long, slender build

AT A GLANCE

✔ Long, slender build
✔ Chubby face with tiny ears
✔ Short, smooth fur
✔ Plain back

Similar-looking families Behaviourally, otters resemble the water mongoose, but the latter has a longer, shaggier coat and a thinner, pointier face.

Badger, polecat and weasel (go to p.93)

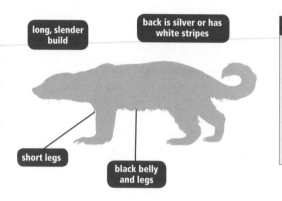

long, slender build

back is silver or has white stripes

short legs

black belly and legs

AT A GLANCE

✔ Short legs
✔ Long, slender build
✔ Back is silver or has white stripes
✔ Black belly and legs

Similar-looking families Mongooses superficially resemble the African striped weasel, but lack the striking black-and-white coat.

Primates (go to p.95)

typical primate-like hands and feet

AT A GLANCE

✔ Typical primate-like hands and feet

White rhinos fall into the distinctive mammals visual group.

Distinctive mammals

The mammals in this group are iconic and require little introduction. They are included because you are likely to encounter them when visiting game reserves and because no book on southern African mammals would be complete without them. Pointers are given only to distinguish between the white and black rhinos.

In the accounts that follow, most of the size measurements given are averages. Separate male and female height and weight measurements are specified only when there is a marked difference between the sexes.

Elephant families are headed by a matriarch.

DISTINCTIVE MAMMALS HAVE TWO VISUAL GROUPS

Distinctive mammals excluding rhinos
African elephant, hippopotamus, giraffe, porcupine, southern African hedgehog, aardvark and ground pangolin.

Rhinos
White rhino and black rhino.

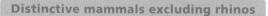

African (savanna) elephant
Afrikaanse olifant
Loxodonta africana

Hippopotamus
Seekoei
Hippopotamus amphibius

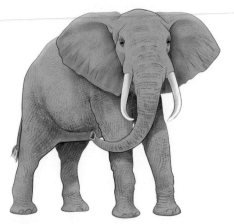

Height 1.5m **Weight** 1.5t
Habitat Most bodies of fresh water, provided they are still or slow-moving. Ventures out of the water to sunbathe and graze.
Habits Spends much of the day in or near water. Emerges and ventures further afield at night in order to feed. In family groups led by a dominant male that aggressively defends his herd and territory. Considered by many to be Africa's most dangerous mammal.

Height male, 3.4m; female, 2.7m
Weight male, 5.5t; female, 3.5t
Habitat A wide range, including bushveld, desert, forest and coastal vegetation.
Habits Highly social. Family groups are led by an older cow (the matriarch) and include her offspring, other cows and their young. Teenage males are expelled from the herd and may be solitary or form bachelor groups. Older males tend to be solitary. Generally calm, but dangerous when provoked (particularly bulls in musth).

AT A GLANCE
Similar species None.

NOTE A small number of African elephants still live in the Knysna forest. Some elephant populations also occur in desert habitat.

AT A GLANCE
Similar species None.

Giraffe
Kameelperd
Giraffa camelopardalis

Height 3m **Weight** 1.1t
Habitat Woodland.
Habits Often in loose
groups of females and
their young. Adult
males mostly solitary,
except when paired
with females
in oestrus.

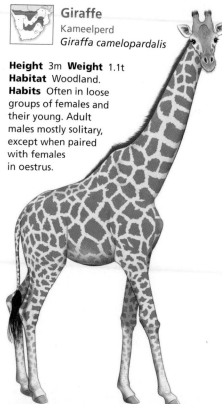

AT A GLANCE

Similar species None.

NOTE Mature males tend to be larger and darker
than females.

Porcupine
Ystervark
Hystrix africaeaustralis

Length 85cm **Weight** 13.5kg
Habitat A wide range throughout the region,
but absent from the Namibian coast.
Habits Nocturnal. Remains in burrows or
among thick vegetation by day.

AT A GLANCE

Similar species None. The
long black-and-white quills
are distinctive.

Southern African hedgehog
Suid-Afrikaanse krimpvarkie
Atelerix frontalis

Length 18cm **Weight** 320g
Habitat Wide-ranging, but avoids wet areas.
Requires some cover.
Habits Predominantly nocturnal. Mostly
solitary, although mothers may be accompanied
by their young. Hedgehogs curl up into a ball
when threatened.

AT A GLANCE

Similar species None. The tiny body
covered in short quills is distinctive.

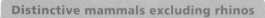

Aardvark (Antbear)

Aardvark
Orycteropus afer

Ground pangolin

Ietermagog
Manis temminckii

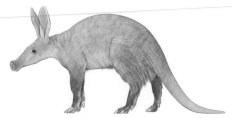

Length 1.6m **Weight** 52kg
Habitat Grassland, scrub and woodland, but less likely to be encountered in dense forest.
Habits Nocturnal. Usually solitary, although females are sometimes seen with a single young.

Length 80cm **Weight** 12kg
Habitat Open woodland and savanna.
Habits Predominantly nocturnal, but occasionally seen during the day. Usually solitary, but a mother may be accompanied by a single young. When threatened, may roll up into a defensive ball.

Arid Kalahari savanna vegetation is suitable habitat for the ground pangolin.

AT A GLANCE

Similar species None.

AT A GLANCE

Similar species None.

Black (hook-lipped) rhino

Swartrenoster
Diceros bicornis

White (square-lipped) rhino

Witrenoster
Ceratotherium simum

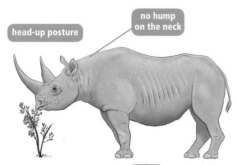

head-up posture
no hump on the neck

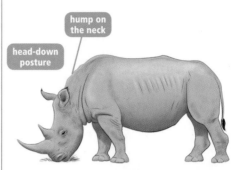

hump on the neck
head-down posture

Height 1.5m
Weight 850kg
Habitat Woodland
with both shrubs and trees.
Never far from water.
Habits Mostly solitary, although
mothers may be accompanied by
their young. More aggressive than the
white rhino.

pointed upper lip

Height 1.8m
Weight male, 2.1t;
female, 1.6t
Habitat Savanna and open
woodland. Requires trees for
cover, edible grass and access
to water.
Habits Females usually solitary or
with young. Males almost always solitary. Groups
may gather and feed together where food is
abundant. More placid than the black rhino.

squared-off upper lip

HZ / WC

DN

AT A GLANCE

✔ Head-up posture
✔ No hump on the neck
✔ Pointed upper lip

Similar species White rhino
distinguished by square top lip,
adapted for grazing, and the hump
on the neck.

NOTE Young black rhino may lack a horn and is
always accompanied by its parents.

AT A GLANCE

✔ Head-down posture
✔ Hump on the neck
✔ Squared-off upper lip

Similar species Black rhino,
distinguished by pointier upper lip,
used for browsing, and the absence
of a hump on the neck.

NOTE Young white rhino may lack horn. Always
accompanied by its mother.

Antelope and buffalo

While antelope often pose identification challenges, there are some features that help in distinguishing them. For example, almost all male antelope have horns and these are often species-specific, providing one of the easiest ways to identify an antelope. Horn shape, size and length are important, as are details such as ridges and horn tips, which may point upward, inward, backward or forward.

Further, markings on the face, belly, rump, sides, forelegs and tail can also be diagnostic in antelope and should be observed carefully. All antelope are diurnal.

Note the following:

- Because their bellies can vary in colour, the male and female Sharpe's grysbok and the male and female common duikers have multiple entries and occur in **both** the 'white belly' and 'belly not white' groups.

- Although the impala and the black-faced impala are in fact subspecies, not fully separate species, their appearance differs sufficiently for them to be treated separately in this book. The same applies to the blesbok and bontebok.

- In a number of species male and female fall into separate visual groups.

> ### 🔭 LOOK FOR
>
> ✔ **Presence or absence of horns**
> ✔ **Presence or absence of ridges on the horns**
> ✔ **Horn shape**
> ✔ **Pointing direction of horn tips**
> ✔ **Markings on coat, tail and/ or legs**
> ✔ **Belly colour**
> ✔ **Bridge of muzzle's colour**
> ✔ **Shape and length of ears**
> ✔ **Distribution**

ANTELOPE ARE DIVIDED INTO EIGHT VISUAL GROUPS

Prominently ridged, curved horns; white belly (go to p.22)

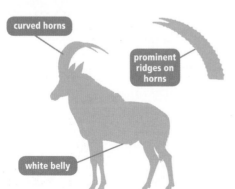

curved horns

prominent ridges on horns

white belly

Prominently ridged, curved horns; belly not white (go to p.28)

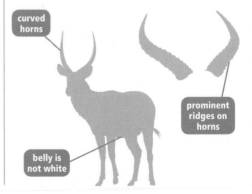

curved horns

prominent ridges on horns

belly is not white

SEPARATING VISUAL GROUPS

No horns; white belly; medium size
(go to p.30)

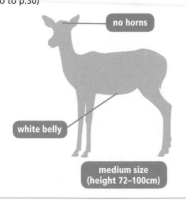

no horns

white belly

medium size
(height 72–100cm)

No horns; white belly; small size
(go to p.34)

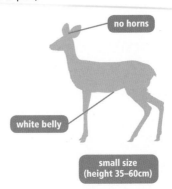

no horns

white belly

small size
(height 35–60cm)

No horns; belly not white (go to p.38)

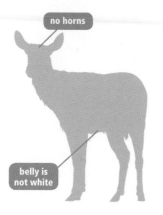

no horns

belly is
not white

Horns not straight, indistinct
or no ridges (go to p.42)

horns lack
prominent
ridges

horns are not
straight

Straight horns; belly not white
(go to p.46)

straight
horns

belly is not white

Straight horns; white belly (go to p.49)

straight
horns

white belly

Roan
Bastergemsbok
Hippotragus equinus

Sable
Swartwitpens
Hippotragus niger

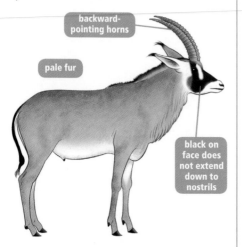

backward-pointing horns

pale fur

black on face does not extend down to nostrils

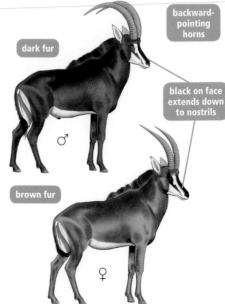

backward-pointing horns

dark fur

black on face extends down to nostrils

♂

brown fur

♀

Height 1.45m **Weight** 260kg
Habitat Open or lightly wooded grassland.
Requires water in its habitat.
Habits In small groups led by a dominant
male. Young males usually form bachelor herds.
Mature bulls outside a herd tend to be solitary.

Height 1.3m **Weight** 220kg
Habitat Savanna woodland. Never strays too far
from water.
Habits In small herds of females and their
young led by a dominant male who may patrol
his territory and repel invading males. Younger
males form small bachelor herds.

AT A GLANCE

Male
✔ Dark fur
✔ Backward-pointing horns
✔ Black on face extends down to nostrils

Female
✔ Brown fur
✔ Backward-pointing horns
✔ Black on face extends down to nostrils

Similar species Male is distinctive,
with black fur. Female may
resemble roan (alongside), but is a
darker chocolate brown.

AT A GLANCE

✔ Pale fur
✔ Backward-pointing horns
✔ Black on face does not extend down
to nostrils

Similar species Sable (alongside)
females tend to be much darker
than the roan.

Impala (male)
Rooibok
Aepyceros melampus melampus

 ## Black-faced impala (male)
Swartneus-rooibok
Aepyceros melampus petersi

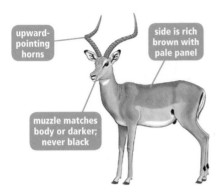

- upward-pointing horns
- side is rich brown with pale panel
- muzzle matches body or darker; never black

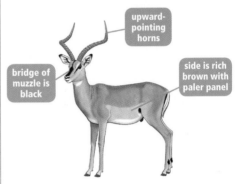

- upward-pointing horns
- bridge of muzzle is black
- side is rich brown with paler panel

Height 90cm **Weight** 55kg
Habitat Woodland with easy access to water. Avoids dense or very exposed habitats.
Habits Usually in herds of about 20 animals, but may congregate in far greater numbers to feed. Adult males form bachelor herds outside the breeding season.

Height 90cm **Weight** 64kg
Habitat Woodland, especially dense habitat. Always remains within reach of water.
Habits Usually in herds of about 20 animals, but may congregate in far greater numbers to feed. Adult males form bachelor herds outside the breeding season.

AT A GLANCE

✔ Muzzle matches body or darker; never black
✔ Upward-pointing horns
✔ Side is rich brown with pale panel

 Similar species Black-faced impala (alongside) has black markings on the bridge of its muzzle. Springbok (p.27) is distinguished by its dark side panel. Red lechwe's (pp.24, 31) sides are uniform or graduated from rich to light brown, and it occurs in different habitat. **See female p.30.**

AT A GLANCE

✔ Upward-pointing horns
✔ Side is rich brown with paler panel
✔ Bridge of muzzle is black

 Similar species Impala (alongside and p.30) has paler muzzle bridge. Springbok (p.27) has a dark side stripe. Red lechwe's (pp.24, 31) sides are uniform or graduated from rich to light brown, and it occurs in different habitat. **See female p.30.**

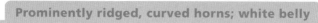

Red lechwe (male)
Rooi-lechwe
Kobus leche

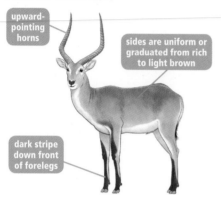

upward-pointing horns

sides are uniform or graduated from rich to light brown

dark stripe down front of forelegs

Height 1m **Weight** 115kg
Habitat Swamps, as well as seasonally and permanently wet grasslands.
Habits Small herds of up to five animals led by a dominant male. Sometimes gathers in large groups to feed.

AT A GLANCE

✔ Upward-pointing horns
✔ Sides are uniform or graduated from rich to light brown
✔ Dark stripe down front of forelegs

Similar species Impala (pp.23, 30) has clearly defined pale side panel. Springbok (p.27) has dark side stripe. Puku (alongside and p.31) and southern mountain reedbuck (opposite and p.32) lack the dark line on forelegs. Southern reedbuck (opposite and p.32) has forward-pointing horns. **See female p.31.**

Puku (male)
Poekoe
Kobus vardonii

upward-pointing horns

uniform golden brown sides

forelegs are paler in front

Height 80cm **Weight** 75kg
Habitat Within southern Africa it is restricted to the Chobe flood plain.
Habits Usually in small herds led by a dominant male. Occasionally larger groups congregate and feed together.

AT A GLANCE

✔ Forelegs are paler in front
✔ Upward-pointing horns
✔ Uniform golden brown sides

Similar species Both reedbuck species (opposite and p.32) have forward-pointing horns. Springbok (p.27) and impala (pp.23, 30) have clearly defined side panels. Red lechwe (alongside and p.31) has dark foreleg stripe. **See female p.31.**

Southern reedbuck (male)
Rietbok
Redunca arundinum

gently curving horns

forward-pointing horns

dark line down front of forelegs

Height 90cm **Weight** 52kg
Habitat Lush, tall grassland near water, for instance in wetlands.
Habits Typically feeds at night. Usually alone or in pairs, but sometimes in small groups.

AT A GLANCE

✔ Dark line down front of forelegs
✔ Gently curving horns
✔ Forward-pointing horns

Similar species Southern mountain reedbuck (alongside and p.32) lacks the dark line on front of forelegs. All other species in this group have upward- or backward-pointing horns. **See female p.32.**

Southern mountain reedbuck (male)
Rooiribbok
Redunca fulvorufula

forward-pointing horns

sharply curving horns

no dark line down front of forelegs

Height 75cm **Weight** 30kg
Habitat Stony slopes in hilly areas with some grass and scattered bush for cover.
Habits In small herds dominated by a single male. Young males are solitary or form small bachelor groups.

AT A GLANCE

✔ No dark line down front of forelegs
✔ Sharply curving horns
✔ Forward-pointing horns

Similar species Southern reedbuck (alongside and p.32) has dark line on front of forelegs. All other similar antelope have backward- or upward-pointing horns. **See female p.32.**

Bontebok

Bontebok
Damaliscus pygargus pygargus

Blesbok

Blesbok
Damaliscus pygargus phillipsi

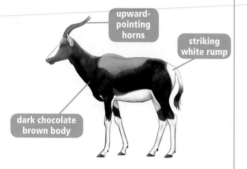

upward-pointing horns

striking white rump

dark chocolate brown body

upward-pointing horns

pale, not white, rump

chocolate brown body

Height 90cm **Weight** 60kg
Habitat Mixed grassland and fynbos.
Habits Adult males are territorial. Females and their young move in small herds. Young males often form bachelor herds.

Height 95cm **Weight** 70kg
Habitat Grassland near water.
Habits Adult males may dominate small to large herds of females during breeding season. Young males form bachelor herds.

AT A GLANCE

✔ Dark chocolate brown body
✔ Upward-pointing horns
✔ Striking white rump

Similar species Sable (p.22) has long, backward-curved horns and totally different distribution. Blesbok (alongside) has pale, but not white, rump and totally different distribution; its facial blaze is often, but not always, discontinuous.

AT A GLANCE

✔ Chocolate brown body
✔ Upward-pointing horns
✔ Pale, not white, rump

Similar species Sable (p.22) has strongly backward-curving horns and different distribution. Bontebok (alongside) has a much more striking white rump and different distribution, and the facial blaze is often continuous, although not invariably.

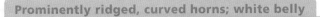

Springbok

Springbok
Antidorcas marsupialis

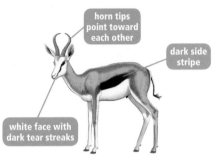

horn tips point toward each other

dark side stripe

white face with dark tear streaks

Height male, 75cm; female, 60cm
Weight male, 40kg; female, 38kg
Habitat Favours arid and semi-arid karoo vegetation, as well as grassland. Almost exclusively confined to wide, flat plains.
Habits The national animal of South Africa. In herds of up to 200 animals, although migrant herds once numbered hundreds of thousands. Males are known for 'pronking' – springing high into the air – to attract females.

GK

AT A GLANCE

✔ White face with dark tear streaks
✔ Horn tips point toward each other
✔ Dark side stripe

Similar species Male impala (p.23) and red lechwe (pp.24, 31) both have longer, more spiralling horns. Male impala has pale side panel. Red lechwe also occurs in different habitat and its sides are uniform or graduated from rich to light brown.

Typical habitats for this visual group

DN

Impala (p.23) favour bushveld habitat.

DN

Mountainous grassland is the ideal habitat for southern mountain reedbuck (p.25).

DN

Red lechwe (p.24) and southern reedbuck (p.25) both occur in wetland areas, like that shown here.

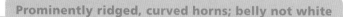

Waterbuck (male)
Waterbok
Kobus ellipsiprymnus

Tsessebe
Tsessebe
Damaliscus lunatus

horn tips point upward

white ring on rump

prominent white on throat

horn tips point upward

no white ring on rump

lacks prominent white on throat

Height 1.6m **Weight** 260kg
Habitat Reed beds, grassland and woodland. Never strays far from water.
Habits Mature males establish territories through which medium-sized herds of females and young wander. Males without a territory tend to form bachelor herds.

Height 1.3m **Weight** 135kg
Habitat Woodland and surrounding grassland, often near water.
Habits Small male-dominated herds of females and young. Single males form bachelor herds. When food is plentiful, larger groups may form.

AT A GLANCE

✔ White ring on rump
✔ Horn tips point upward
✔ Prominent white on throat

Similar species None. The white ring on the rump is diagnostic.
See female p.41.

AT A GLANCE

✔ Lacks prominent white on throat
✔ Horn tips point upward
✔ No white ring on rump

Similar species In both of the hartebeest species (opposite) the horn tips point backward.

Lichtenstein's hartebeest

Mofhartebees
Alcelaphus lichtensteinii

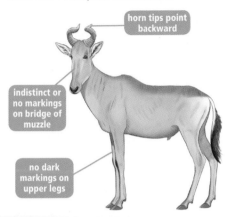

horn tips point backward

indistinct or no markings on bridge of muzzle

no dark markings on upper legs

Height 1.25m **Weight** 170kg
Habitat Savanna, but may stray into grassland. Dependent on water.
Habits When grazing conditions are good, large herds gather. Otherwise in smaller herds of females and their young, dominated by a single male. Bachelor males form herds.

Red hartebeest

Rooihartebees
Alcelaphus buselaphus

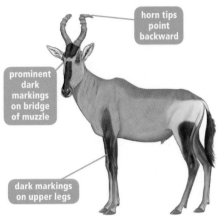

horn tips point backward

prominent dark markings on bridge of muzzle

dark markings on upper legs

Height 1.3m **Weight** 150kg
Habitat Grassland and savanna. Less common in woodland. Among the few antelope species that does not require drinking water.
Habits A dominant male leads a small herd of females and young, as is typical of many antelope species. Bachelor males form herds.

AT A GLANCE

✔ No dark markings on upper legs
✔ Indistinct or no markings on bridge of muzzle
✔ Horn tips point backward

Similar species Tsessebe (opposite) has upward-pointing horns. Red hartebeest (alongside) has black markings on the legs and a black blaze on the muzzle.

AT A GLANCE

✔ Dark markings on upper legs
✔ Prominent dark markings on bridge of muzzle
✔ Horn tips point backward

Similar species Lichtenstein's hartebeest (alongside) lacks dark markings on the legs and forehead. Tsessebe (opposite) has upward-pointing horns.

Impala (female)

Rooibok
Aepyceros melampus melampus

Black-faced impala (female)
Swartneus-rooibok
Aepyceros melampus petersi

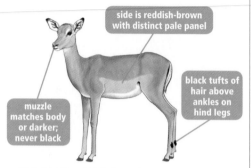

side is reddish-brown with distinct pale panel

black tufts of hair above ankles on hind legs

muzzle matches body or darker; never black

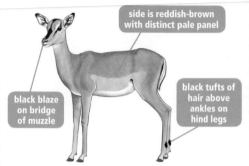

side is reddish-brown with distinct pale panel

black blaze on bridge of muzzle

black tufts of hair above ankles on hind legs

Height 85cm **Weight** 40kg
Habitat Woodland, always within reach of water. Avoids dense habitat.
Habits Usually in herds of around 20 animals, but may congregate in much larger numbers to feed. Territorial males form bachelor herds outside the breeding season.

Height 90cm **Weight** 50kg
Habitat Woodland, always within reach of water. Avoids dense habitat.
Habits Usually in herds of around 20 animals, but may congregate in much larger numbers to feed. Territorial males form bachelor herds out of the breeding season.

AT A GLANCE

✔ Muzzle matches body or darker; never black
✔ Side is reddish-brown with distinct pale panel
✔ Black tufts of hair above ankles on hind legs

Similar species Grey rhebok (pp.33, 49) and both reedbuck species (pp.25, 32) have greyer coats. Black-faced impala (alongside and p.23) has black muzzle bridge. Puku and red lechwe (pp.24 and opposite) both lack the clearly defined side panel. **See male p.23.**

AT A GLANCE

✔ Black blaze on bridge of muzzle
✔ Side is reddish-brown with distinct pale panel
✔ Black tufts of hair above ankles on hind legs

Similar species Grey rhebok (pp.33, 49) and both reedbuck species (pp.25, 32) have greyer coats. Impala's (alongside) muzzle bridge is pale, matching its body. Puku and red lechwe (p.24 and opposite) both lack the clearly defined side panel. **See male p.23.**

Red lechwe (female)
Rooi-lechwe
Kobus leche

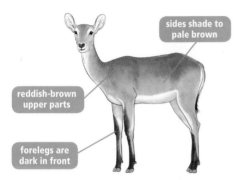

sides shade to pale brown

reddish-brown upper parts

forelegs are dark in front

Height 95cm **Weight** 75kg
Habitat Typically flooded grassland. Never strays far from water.
Habits In small herds of up to five animals led by a dominant male. May gather in larger groups to feed.

SJ / WC

Similar species Grey rhebok (pp.33, 49) and both reedbuck species (pp.25, 32) have much greyer coats. Both impala species (opposite and p.23) have clearly defined side panels. Puku (alongside and p.24) lacks darker foreleg markings. **See male p.24.**

Puku (female)
Poekoe
Kobus vardonii

reddish-brown coat

sides lack obvious panel

forelegs lack dark markings

Height 75cm **Weight** 60kg
Habitat Within southern Africa it is restricted to the Chobe flood plain.
Habits Usually in small herds led by a dominant male. May gather in larger groups to feed.

HH / WC

Similar species Grey rhebok (pp.33, 49) and both reedbuck species (pp.25, 32) have much greyer coats. Both impala species (opposite and p.23) have clearly defined side panels. Red lechwe (alongside and p.24) has dark markings on the front of its forelegs. **See male p.24.**

Southern reedbuck (female)
Rietbok
Redunca arundinum

Southern mountain reedbuck (female)
Rooiribbok
Redunca fulvorufula

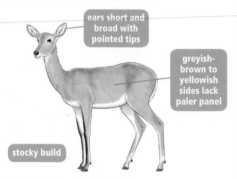

ears short and broad with pointed tips

greyish-brown to yellowish sides lack paler panel

stocky build

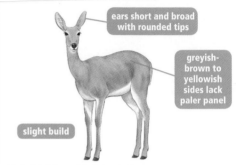

ears short and broad with rounded tips

greyish-brown to yellowish sides lack paler panel

slight build

Height 80cm **Weight** 70kg
Habitat Long, lush grass near water, for example in wetlands.
Habits Feeds at night, unlike other members of this group. Usually solitary or in pairs, but sometimes in small groups.

Height 70cm **Weight** 25kg
Habitat Stony slopes with grass and scattered bush in hilly habitat.
Habits In small herds led by a single male. Young and bachelor males live alone or in small bachelor groups.

This scene shows typical southern reedbuck habitat.

AT A GLANCE

✔ Stocky build
✔ Ears short and broad with pointed tips
✔ Greyish-brown to yellowish sides lack paler panel

Similar species Puku and red lechwe (pp.24, 31) and impala (pp.23, 30) all have much richer, reddish-brown coats. Southern mountain reedbuck (p.25 and alongside) is slightly built and less than half the weight. Grey rhebok (opposite and p.49) has much longer, thinner ears. **See male p.25.**

AT A GLANCE

✔ Slight build
✔ Ears short and broad with rounded tips
✔ Greyish-brown to yellowish sides lack paler panel

Similar species Puku and red lechwe (pp.24, 31) and impala (pp.23, 30) all have much richer, reddish-brown coats. Southern reedbuck (p.25 and alongside) is stockier and more than double the weight. Grey rhebok (opposite and p.49) has much longer, thinner ears. **See male p.25.**

Grey rhebok (female)
Vaalribbok
Pelea capreolus

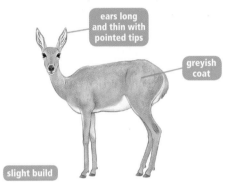

ears long and thin with pointed tips

greyish coat

slight build

Height 75cm **Weight** 25kg
Habitat Favours alpine slopes and hilly areas with good grass cover.
Habits A dominant male defends a small herd. Bachelor males are solitary.

AT A GLANCE
✔ Slight build
✔ Ears long and thin with pointed tips
✔ Greyish coat

Similar species Puku and red lechwe (pp.24, 31) and impala (pp.23, 30) all have reddish-brown coats. Both reedbuck species (p.25 and opposite) have much shorter ears. **See male p.49.**

Typical habitats for this visual group

Bushveld vegetation provides ideal habitat for impala (p.30).

Grey rhebok (alongside) occur on slopes along the Drakensberg escarpment.

Several antelope in this group occur in wetland areas.

Steenbok (female)
Steenbok
Raphicerus campestris

Oribi (female)
Oorbietjie
Ourebia ourebi

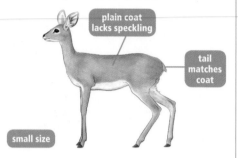

plain coat lacks speckling

tail matches coat

small size

tail black above, white below

bridge of muzzle matches coat colour

small size

Height 52cm **Weight** 12kg
Habitat Tall grassland with scattered bush. Avoids rocky and mountainous areas. Not dependent on water.
Habits Usually solitary, but sometimes in pairs.

Height 60cm **Weight** 14kg
Habitat Grassland with scattered bush and thicket.
Habits In small herds led by a dominant male.

GMS, FWS / WC

AT A GLANCE
✔ Small size
✔ Plain coat lacks speckling
✔ Tail matches coat

Similar species Damara dik-dik (pp.36, 52) and suni (opposite and p.50) are noticeably smaller. Common duiker (opposite and p.53) and oribi (alongside and p.51) both have black on tail. Sharpe's grysbok (pp.36, 40, 46, 52) is the only species in this group with white streaks on entire coat. Klipspringer (pp.37, 50) has different coat markings and inhabits rocky habitat. **See male p.51.**

AT A GLANCE
✔ Small size
✔ Bridge of muzzle matches coat colour
✔ Tail black above, white below

Similar species Damara dik-dik (pp.36, 52) and suni (opposite and p.50) are far smaller. Klipspringer (pp.37, 50) and steenbok (alongisde and p.51) have tails that match coat colour. Oribi distinguished by the colour on the bridge of its muzzle. Sharpe's grysbok (pp.36, 40, 46, 52) is the only species in this group with white streaks on entire coat. **See male p.51.**

Suni (female)

Soenie
Neotragus moschatus

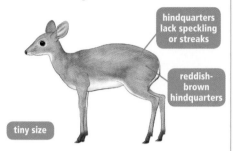

hindquarters lack speckling or streaks

reddish-brown hindquarters

tiny size

Height 35cm **Weight** 6kg
Habitat Ranges from woodland to denser habitats and riverine bush. Not dependent on water.
Habits Almost always solitary or in pairs, sometimes with young. Both males and females are territorial.

AT A GLANCE

✔ Tiny size
✔ Hindquarters lack speckling or streaks
✔ Reddish-brown hindquarters

Similar species Common duiker (alongside and p.53), steenbok and oribi (opposite and p.51), and klipspringer (pp.37, 50) are all far bigger. Damara dik-dik (pp.36, 52) has greyish hindquarters. Sharpe's grysbok (pp.36, 40, 46, 52) is the only species in this group with entirely white-streaked coat. **See male p.50.**

Common (grey) duiker (female no horns)

Gewone duiker
Sylvicapra grimmia

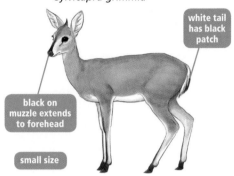

white tail has black patch

black on muzzle extends to forehead

small size

Height 52cm **Weight** 22kg
Habitat Requires scrub and bush for cover. Not dependent on water.
Habits Usually solitary, or, rarely, in breeding pairs. Females may be seen with young.

AT A GLANCE

✔ Small size
✔ Black on muzzle extends to forehead
✔ White tail has black patch

Similar species Damara dik-dik (pp.36, 52) and suni (alongside and p.50) are both noticeably smaller. Klipspringer (pp.37, 50) and steenbok (opposite and p.51) both have tails that match their coat colour. Oribi (opposite and p.51) distinguished by the colour on the muzzle bridge. Sharpe's grysbok (pp.36, 40, 46, 52) is the only species in this group with entirely white-streaked coat. **See male and female with horns p.53.**

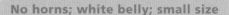

Damara dik-dik (female)
Damara dik-dik
Madoqua damarensis

Sharpe's grysbok (female)
Sharpe se grysbok
Raphicerus sharpei

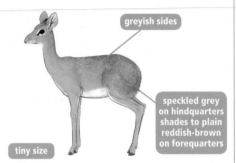

greyish sides

speckled grey on hindquarters shades to plain reddish-brown on forequarters

tiny size

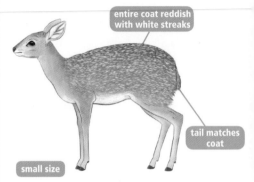

entire coat reddish with white streaks

tail matches coat

small size

Height 39cm **Weight** 5kg
Habitat Dense woodland. Favours open understorey and is not dependent on water.
Habits Usually solitary or in very small family groups. May be more social in the dry season.

Height 50cm **Weight** 9kg
Habitat Favours dense scrub in grassy areas.
Habits Either solitary or in pairs. Females are sometimes seen with young.

AT A GLANCE
✔ Tiny size
✔ Greyish sides
✔ Speckled grey on hindquarters shades to plain reddish-brown on forequarters

Similar species Common duiker (pp.35, 53), steenbok and oribi (pp.34, 51) and klipspringer (opposite and p.50) are all noticeably bigger. Suni (pp.35, 50) has reddish-brown hindquarters. Sharpe's grysbok (alongside and pp.40, 46, 52) is the only species in this group with white streaks on entire coat. **See male p.52.**

AT A GLANCE
✔ Small size
✔ Entire coat reddish with white streaks
✔ Tail matches coat

Similar species Bears some resemblance to all other species in this group, but has entirely white-streaked coat. **See female p.40 and male pp.46 and 52.**

NOTE Belly may not appear white in some individuals, so female is also featured in 'No horns; belly not white'. White streaks may not be visible at a distance.

Klipspringer (female)
Klipspringer
Oreotragus oreotragus

dark speckling on coat

tail matches coat

small size

Height 60cm **Weight** 13kg
Habitat Occurs almost exclusively in rocky areas, as the common name klipspringer, meaning 'rock jumper', suggests. Does not require drinking water.
Habits Often found in pairs. Frequently stands on top of large hillside boulders.

AT A GLANCE

✔ Small size
✔ Dark speckling on coat
✔ Tail matches coat

 Similar species Damara dik-dik (opposite and p.52) and suni (pp.35, 50) are both noticeably smaller. Common duiker (pp.35, 53) and oribi (pp.34, 51) both have black-and-white tails. Steenbok (pp.34, 51) lacks dark speckling and avoids rocky areas. Sharpe's grysbok (opposite and pp.40, 46, 52) is the only species in the group with entirely white-streaked coat. **See male p.50.**

Typical habitats for this visual group

A mixture of scrub and bush provides suitable cover for the common duiker (p.35).

Both steenbok and oribi (p.34) occur in savanna habitat.

The suni (p.35) inhabits riverine bush.

(Greater) kudu (female)
Koedoe
Tragelaphus strepsiceros

 Nyala (female)
Njala
Tragelaphus angasii

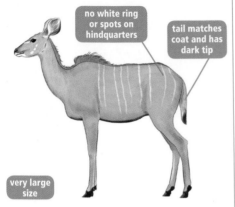

no white ring or spots on hindquarters

tail matches coat and has dark tip

very large size

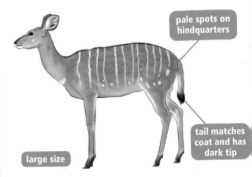

pale spots on hindquarters

tail matches coat and has dark tip

large size

Height 1.3m **Weight** 175kg
Habitat Primarily savanna and woodland. Avoids both very dense and exposed habitats.
Habits In small herds led by a dominant male. Bachelor males may form herds or remain solitary.

Height 95cm **Weight** 60kg
Habitat Favours dense woodland and riverine bush, but may venture into forest.
Habits In small to medium-sized herds led by a dominant male. Young and unpaired males may form bachelor herds.

AT A GLANCE

✔ Very large size
✔ No white ring or spots on hindquarters
✔ Tail matches coat and has dark tip

 Similar species None. Female kudu is distinguished by her size and the absence of spots on her hindquarters. **See male p.42.**

AT A GLANCE

✔ Large size
✔ Pale spots on hindquarters
✔ Tail matches coat and has dark tip

 Similar species Female kudu (alongside) bears a superficial resemblance, but is dramatically larger. Sitatunga female (opposite) has white-tipped tail with a black ring. Bushbuck female (opposite) has white-tipped tail with no black ring. **See male p.42.**

Sitatunga (female)
Waterkoedoe
Tragelaphus spekii

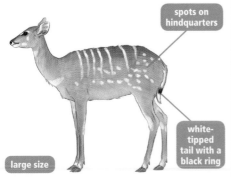

spots on hindquarters

white-tipped tail with a black ring

large size

Height 90cm **Weight** 55kg
Habitat Usually in or around wetlands, but sometimes in grassland. Never far from water.
Habits In small herds led by a dominant male. Males without a territory usually live alone.

AT A GLANCE

✔ Large size
✔ Spots on hindquarters
✔ White-tipped tail with a black ring

Similar species Female kudu (opposite) bears superficial resemblance, but size difference is dramatic. Bushbuck female (alongside) has white-tipped tail with no black ring. Nyala female (opposite) has black-tipped tail. **See male p.43.**

Bushbuck (female)
Bosbok
Tragelaphus scriptus

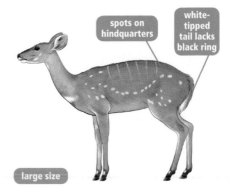

white-tipped tail lacks black ring

spots on hindquarters

large size

Height 70cm **Weight** 33kg
Habitat Dense woodland and forest. Never far from water.
Habits In small herds that may consist of males only, females only, or mixed sexes.

AT A GLANCE

✔ Large size
✔ Spots on hindquarters
✔ White-tipped tail lacks black ring

Similar species Female kudu (opposite) bears superficial resemblance, but size difference is dramatic. Sitatunga female (alongside) has white-tipped tail with a black ring. Nyala female (opposite) has black-tipped tail. **See male p.43.**

Sharpe's grysbok (female)
Sharpe se grysbok
Raphicerus sharpei

(Cape) grysbok (female)
Grysbok
Raphicerus melanotis

reddish coat with white streaks

tiny size

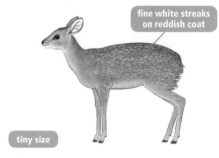

fine white streaks on reddish coat

tiny size

Height 50cm **Weight** 9kg
Habitat Favours dense scrub in grassy areas.
Habits Either solitary or in pairs. Females sometimes seen with young.

Height 54cm **Weight** 10kg
Habitat Dense fynbos, scrub and even bushy habitats.
Habits Almost always solitary, except when females are accompanied by young.

AT A GLANCE
✔ Distribution
✔ Tiny size
✔ Reddish coat with white streaks

Similar species Grysbok (alongside and p.46) is similar size, but has darker belly and different distribution. All others in this group are significantly larger. **See female p.36 and male pp.46 and 52.**

NOTE Belly may appear white in some individuals, so female Sharpe's grysbok is also featured in 'No horns; white belly; small size'. White streaks may not be visible at a distance.

AT A GLANCE
✔ Distribution
✔ Tiny size
✔ Fine white streaks on reddish coat

Similar species Sharpe's grysbok (p.36 and alongside and pp.46, 52) is similar size, but has paler belly and different distribution. All others in this group are significantly larger. **See male p.46.**

NOTE White streaks may not be visible at a distance.

Waterbuck (female)
Waterbok
Kobus ellipsiprymnus

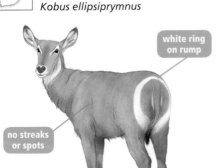

white ring on rump

no streaks or spots

very large size

Height 1.2m **Weight** 220kg
Habitat Wide ranging, including woodland and the margins of wetlands. Never far from water.
Habits In small to medium-sized herds led by a single male. Bachelor males may be solitary or form herds.

AT A GLANCE

✔ Very large size
✔ No streaks or spots
✔ White ring on rump

Similar species None. The white ring on the rump is diagnostic.
See male p.28.

Typical habitats for this visual group

A kudu (p.38) in ideal woodland habitat.

Many members of this group occur in riverine woodland.

(Greater) kudu (male)
Koedoe
Tragelaphus strepsiceros

Nyala (male)
Njala
Tragelaphus angasii

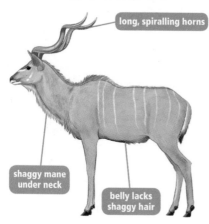

long, spiralling horns

shaggy mane under neck

belly lacks shaggy hair

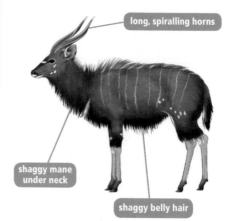

long, spiralling horns

shaggy mane under neck

shaggy belly hair

Height 1.4m **Weight** 230kg
Habitat Primarily savanna and woodland. Avoids both very dense and exposed habitats.
Habits In small herds led by a dominant male. Bachelor males may be solitary or form herds.

Height 1.1m **Weight** 110kg
Habitat Dense woodland and riverine bush. May venture into forest.
Habits In small to medium-sized herds led by a dominant male. Young and unpaired males may form bachelor herds.

AT A GLANCE

✔ Shaggy mane under neck
✔ Long, spiralling horns
✔ Belly lacks shaggy hair

Similar species Sitatunga male (opposite) is significantly smaller with no shaggy mane under the neck. Nyala male (alongside) is smaller and has shaggy mane under the neck and belly. **See female p.38.**

AT A GLANCE

✔ Shaggy mane under neck
✔ Long, spiralling horns
✔ Shaggy belly hair

Similar species Kudu male (alongside) is significantly larger and lacks the shaggy belly hair. Sitatunga male (opposite) lacks shaggy mane under the neck and belly. **See female p.38.**

Sitatunga (male)
Waterkoedoe
Tragelaphus spekii

Bushbuck (male)
Bosbok
Tragelaphus scriptus

long, spiralling horns

no shaggy mane under neck

large size

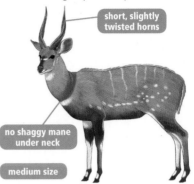

short, slightly twisted horns

no shaggy mane under neck

medium size

Height 90cm **Weight** 110kg
Habitat Usually in or around wetlands, but sometimes in grassland. Never far from water.
Habits In small herds led by a dominant male. Males without a territory live alone.

Height 80cm **Weight** 40kg
Habitat Dense woodland and forest. Never strays far from water.
Habits In small herds comprising males only, females only, or mixed sexes.

AT A GLANCE
✔ Large size
✔ No shaggy mane under neck
✔ Long, spiralling horns

Similar species Kudu male (opposite) bears superficial resemblance, but sitatunga is significantly smaller with a shaggier coat. Nyala male (opposite) has a shaggy mane under the neck. **See female p.39.**

NOTE On close observation you may see that the sitatunga has a white-tipped tail with a black ring, while the bushbuck male has a white-tipped tail with no black ring.

AT A GLANCE
✔ Medium size
✔ No shaggy mane under neck
✔ Short, slightly twisted horns

Similar species Sitatunga's (alongside) coat is shaggier. Nyala (opposite) has shaggy mane under the neck. **See female p.39.**

NOTE Close observation reveals that the bushbuck male has a white-tipped tail with no black ring, while the sitatunga male has a white-tipped tail with a black ring.

Black wildebeest
Swartwildebees
Connochaetes gnou

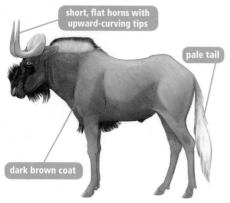

short, flat horns with upward-curving tips

pale tail

dark brown coat

Height 1.1m **Weight** 140kg
Habitat Primarily arid karoo, but requires grass and water in its habitat. Has been reintroduced to Highveld reserves.
Habits In small to medium-sized herds led by a dominant male. Other males may be solitary or form bachelor herds.

AT A GLANCE
✔ Dark brown coat
✔ Short, flat horns with upward-curving tips
✔ Pale tail

Similar species African buffalo (opposite) bears very superficial resemblance, but is significantly larger with a black tail. Blue wildebeest (alongside) has pale blue-grey coat and black tail and its horn bases point outward.

Blue wildebeest
Blouwildebees
Connochaetes taurinus

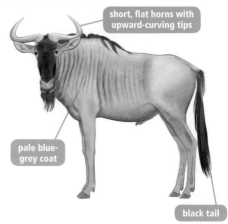

short, flat horns with upward-curving tips

pale blue-grey coat

black tail

Height 1.2m **Weight** 195kg
Habitat Varied, including grassland, woodland and savanna. Dependent on water.
Habits In small to medium-sized herds led by a dominant male. Other males may be solitary or form bachelor herds.

AT A GLANCE
✔ Pale blue-grey coat
✔ Short, flat horns with upward-curving tips
✔ Black tail

Similar species African buffalo (opposite) bears very superficial resemblance, but is significantly larger. Black wildebeest (alongside) has dark brown coat and pale tail and its horn bases point forward.

African buffalo
Buffel
Syncerus caffer

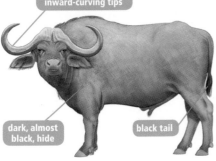

short, flat horns with inward-curving tips

dark, almost black, hide

black tail

Height 1.4m **Weight** 600kg
Habitat Grassland with some scattered trees. Requires grass and water in its habitat.
Habits Most often in large herds, but lone animals and small bachelor herds may be encountered. Can be aggressive during the mating season. Will form an attacking line to charge predators.

AT A GLANCE

✔ Dark, almost black, hide.
✔ Short, flat horns with inward-curving tips
✔ Black tail

 Similar species None. The massive, bulky build and fearsome, flat, curving horns are distinctive.

Typical habitats for this visual group

Open savanna like that shown here is suitable habitat for the African buffalo (alongside).

Rolling Highveld grassland is ideal habitat for black wildebeest (opposite).

Many antelope species occur in riverine habitats like this one.

(Cape) grysbok (male)
Grysbok
Raphicerus melanotis

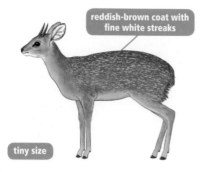

reddish-brown coat with fine white streaks

tiny size

Height 54cm **Weight** 10kg
Habitat Dense fynbos, scrub and even some bushy habitat.
Habits Almost always solitary, except when female is accompanied by her young. Seldom seen.

CMS

AT A GLANCE
✔ Distribution
✔ Tiny size
✔ Reddish-brown coat with fine white streaks

Similar species Sharpe's grysbok (pp.36, 40 and alongside and p.52) can be distinguished by its different distribution. Other small members of this group lack white streaks on the coat. **See female p.40.**

Sharpe's grysbok (male)
Sharpe se grysbok
Raphicerus sharpei

reddish-brown coat with fine white streaks

tiny size

Height 47cm **Weight** 7kg
Habitat Favours dense scrub in grassy areas.
Habits Solitary or in pairs. Females may be accompanied by their young.

CMS

AT A GLANCE
✔ Distribution
✔ Tiny size
✔ Reddish-brown coat with fine white streaks

Similar species Superficially like other small members of this group, but all lack white streaks on the coat, bar the grysbok (p.40 and alongside), which is distinguished by its different distribution. **See female pp.36, 40 and male p.52.**

NOTE Belly may appear white in some individuals, so male is also featured in 'Straight horns; white belly'. White streaks may not be visible at a distance.

Red duiker
Rooiduiker
Cephalophus natalensis

Blue duiker
Blouduiker
Philantomba monticola

no fine white streaks on coat

reddish-brown coat

small size

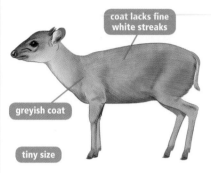

coat lacks fine white streaks

greyish coat

tiny size

Height 40cm **Weight** 12kg
Habitat Favours forest, but sometimes also seen in other dense bushy habitat.
Habits Solitary or in breeding pairs. May be accompanied by young.

Height 30cm **Weight** 4kg
Habitat Favours forest, but sometimes also seen in other dense bushy habitat.
Habits Usually solitary or in breeding pairs. May be accompanied by young.

AT A GLANCE
✔ Small size
✔ Reddish-brown coat
✔ No fine white streaks on coat

Similar species Both grysbok species (opposite and pp.36, 40, 52) bear a superficial resemblance, but have white-streaked coats. Blue duiker's (alongside) coat colour differs.

AT A GLANCE
✔ Tiny size
✔ Greyish coat
✔ Coat lacks fine white streaks

Similar species Both grysbok species (opposite and pp.36, 40, 52) bear a superficial resemblance, but have white-streaked coats. Red duiker's (alongside) coat colour differs.

Eland
Eland
Taurotragus oryx

massive size

Height 1.7 m **Weight** 700kg
Habitat Typically grassland and scrub, but may venture into woodland.
Habits Herd sizes vary greatly and consist of mixed sexes.

AT A GLANCE

✔ Massive size

 Similar species None. No straight-horned antelope is as large or as heavily built as the eland.

Typical habitats for this visual group

Most duiker species (p.47) occupy forest habitat.

Our largest antelope, the eland (alongside), lives in grassland and scrub habitat.

Woodland areas like this are the ideal home for Sharpe's grysbok (p.46).

Gemsbok

Gemsbok
Oryx gazella

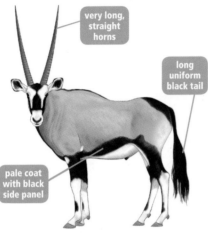

very long, straight horns

long uniform black tail

pale coat with black side panel

Height 1.2m **Weight** 240kg
Habitat Grassland in arid areas. Sometimes ventures into woodland. Not dependent on water and can survive in true desert.
Habits In small herds led by a dominant male. Unpaired males are usually solitary. May form bachelor herds, but this is less common than in other antelope species.

AT A GLANCE

✔ Pale coat with black side panel
✔ Very long, straight horns
✔ Long uniform black tail

Similar species None. The size, long horns and black side panel are distinctive.

Grey rhebok (male)

Vaalribbok
Pelea capreolus

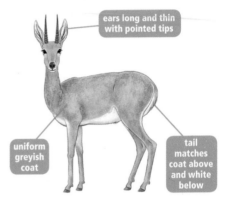

ears long and thin with pointed tips

uniform greyish coat

tail matches coat above and white below

Height 75cm **Weight** 25kg
Habitat Favours alpine slopes and hilly areas with good grass cover.
Habits In small herds defended by a single dominant male. Other males are solitary.

AT A GLANCE

✔ Uniform greyish coat
✔ Ears long and thin with pointed tips
✔ Tail matches coat above and white below

Similar species Superficially similar to other smaller members of this group, but its long ears and larger size are distinctive.
See female p.33.

Klipspringer (male)
Klipspringer
Oreotragus oreotragus

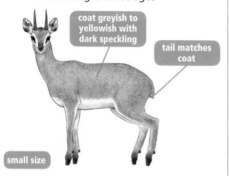

coat greyish to yellowish with dark speckling

tail matches coat

small size

Height 60cm **Weight** 11kg
Habitat As suggested by the name klipspringer, which means 'rock jumper', occurs almost exclusively in rocky areas. Doesn't require drinking water.
Habits Often in pairs. Frequently seen standing on top of large hillside boulders.

AT A GLANCE

✔ Small size
✔ Coat greyish to yellowish with dark speckling
✔ Tail matches coat

Similar species Steenbok (p.34 and opposite), Damara dik-dik (pp.36, 52) and Sharpe's grysbok (pp.36, 40, 46, 52) bear superficial resemblance, but all lack klipspringer's dark speckling. All other species are either larger or have different tail markings. **See female p.37.**

NOTE Where distribution overlaps with steenbok, these species are also separated by favoured habitat.

Suni (male)
Soenie
Neotragus moschatus

uniform reddish coat

tail black above and white below

bridge of muzzle dark

Height 35cm **Weight** 5kg
Habitat Varied. Includes woodland, dense bush and riverine bush. Not dependent on water.
Habits Almost always solitary or in pairs, but sometimes also seen with young. Both male and female are territorial.

AT A GLANCE

✔ Bridge of muzzle dark
✔ Uniform reddish coat
✔ Tail black above and white below

Similar species Common duiker (pp.35, 53) has a greyer coat. Oribi (p.34 and opposite) (although very similar to suni) has muzzle bridge that matches coat colour. All other members of this group are separated by their tail markings. **See female p.35.**

Steenbok (male)

Steenbok
Raphicerus campestris

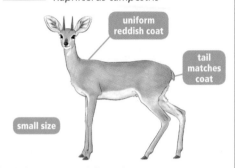

uniform reddish coat

tail matches coat

small size

Height 50cm **Weight** 11kg
Habitat Tall grassland with some scattered bush. Not dependent on water.
Habits Usually solitary, but sometimes in pairs.

AT A GLANCE

✔ Small size
✔ Uniform reddish coat
✔ Tail matches coat

Similar species Klipspringer (p.37 and opposite), Damara dik-dik (pp.36, 52) and Sharpe's grysbok (pp.36, 40, 46, 52) bear superficial resemblance, but all have noticeable coat markings whereas steenbok's coat is uniformly coloured. All other similar species have different tail colouring. **See female p.34.**

Oribi (male)

Oorbietjie
Ourebia ourebi

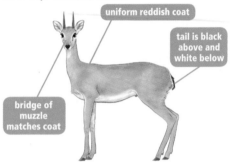

uniform reddish coat

tail is black above and white below

bridge of muzzle matches coat

Height 60cm **Weight** 14kg
Habitat Grassland with thicket and some scattered bush.
Habits In small herds led by a single dominant male.

AT A GLANCE

✔ Bridge of muzzle matches coat
✔ Uniform reddish coat
✔ Tail is black above and white below

Similar species Common duiker (pp. 35, 53) has a greyer coat and dark muzzle bridge. Suni (p.35 and opposite) has a dark muzzle bridge. All other similar species have different tail colouring. **See female p.34.**

Damara dik-dik (male)

Damara dik-dik
Madoqua damarensis

speckled grey rump shades into reddish forequarters

tail matches hind-quarters

tiny size

Height 40cm **Weight** 5kg
Habitat Dense woodland and open understorey. Not dependent on water.
Habits Usually solitary or in very small family groups, but may be more social in the dry season.

AT A GLANCE

✔ Tiny size
✔ Speckled grey rump shades into reddish forequarters
✔ Tail matches hindquarters

Similar species None. The greyish rump that shades into reddish forequarters is distinctive. **See female p.36.**

Sharpe's grysbok (male)

Sharpe se grysbok
Raphicerus sharpei

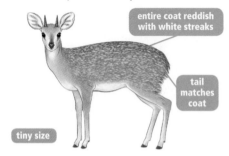

entire coat reddish with white streaks

tail matches coat

tiny size

Height 50cm **Weight** 9kg
Habitat Dense scrub in grassy areas.
Habits Solitary or in pairs. Females sometimes accompanied by their young.

AT A GLANCE

✔ Tiny size
✔ Entire coat reddish with white streaks
✔ Tail matches coat

Similar species Bears some resemblance to other species in this group, but has entirely white-streaked coat. **See female pp.36, 40 and male p.46**

NOTE Belly may not appear white in some individuals, so male also features in 'Straight horns; belly not white'.

Common (grey) duiker
(male and female with horns)
Gewone duiker
Sylvicapra grimmia

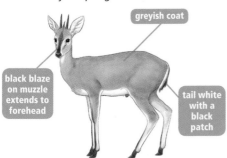

greyish coat

black blaze on muzzle extends to forehead

tail white with a black patch

Height 50cm **Weight** 19kg

Habitat Dense scrub and woodland, provided there is bushy ground cover. Not dependent on water.

Habits Usually solitary, but females may sometimes be accompanied by young. Very rarely seen in breeding pairs.

M / WC

AT A GLANCE

✔ Black blaze on muzzle extends to forehead
✔ Greyish coat
✔ Tail white with a black patch

Similar species Suni (pp.35, 50) and oribi (pp.34, 51) bear superficial resemblance, but have less grey in their coats and the black on their muzzles does not extend to the forehead. All other members of this group are separated by tail colouring. **See female p.35**

NOTE Some females lack horns, so the female common duiker also appears under 'No horns; white belly; small size'.

Typical habitats for this visual group

DN

Gemsbok (p.49) inhabit arid plains like this one.

DN

Check areas of dense woodland for the secretive Sharpe's grysbok (opposite).

GK

Klipspringers (p.50) can be found on large rocky outcrops

Zebras

Members of the zebra family are easily recognised by their horse-like appearance and striped coats. However, distinguishing between different zebra species requires careful observation of the differences in their stripe patterns.

Genetic research has shown that the quagga, which has been extinct for over a century, was a subspecies of plains zebra, and efforts are underway to breed quagga-like plains zebras.

NOTE For the purposes of this guide the two subspecies of mountain zebra, namely the Cape and Hartmann's mountain zebras, are treated separately.

LOOK FOR

✔ belly stripes
✔ presence or absence of shadow stripes
✔ distribution

To tell zebra species apart take careful note of their stripe patterns.

ZEBRAS HAVE ONLY ONE VISUAL GROUP

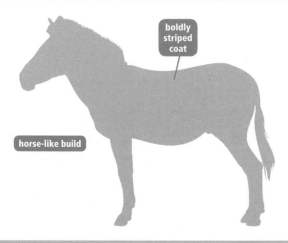

boldly striped coat

horse-like build

Plains zebra

Bontsebra
Equus quagga

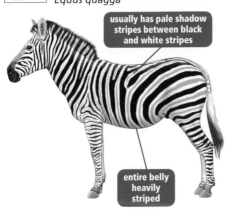

usually has pale shadow stripes between black and white stripes

entire belly heavily striped

Height 1.3m **Weight** 300kg
Habitat Grassland and savanna. Requires drinking water.
Habits Largely diurnal. Usually in family groups led by a dominant male. Bachelor males may form herds.

AT A GLANCE

✔ Entire belly heavily striped
✔ Usually has pale shadow stripes between black and white stripes

 Similar species The two mountain zebras (p.56) bear a superficial resemblance, but are told from plains zebra by their plain white bellies.

This plains zebra is grazing in typical grassland habitat.

Most plains zebras have bolder shadow stripes towards their hindquarters.

Unlike mountain zebras, plains zebras have striped bellies.

Cape mountain zebra
Kaapse bergsebra
Equus zebra zebra

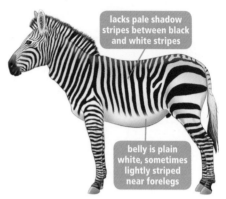

Hartmann's mountain zebra
Hartmann se bergsebra
Equus zebra hartmannae

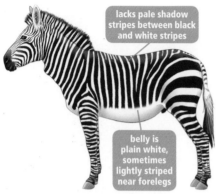

lacks pale shadow stripes between black and white stripes

belly is plain white, sometimes lightly striped near forelegs

Height 1.2m **Weight** 250kg
Habitat Favours mountainous grassland. Avoids bushy habitat. Requires drinking water.
Habits Largely diurnal. Usually in small herds led by a dominant male. Bachelor males form herds.

lacks pale shadow stripes between black and white stripes

belly is plain white, sometimes lightly striped near forelegs

Height 1.5m **Weight** 300kg
Habitat Low mountain slopes. May venture onto adjoining grassy plains, but never strays too far from mountains. Requires drinking water.
Habits Largely diurnal. Usually in small family groups led by a dominant male. Young males may form bachelor herds.

ND / IOA

DN

AT A GLANCE

✔ Distribution
✔ Lacks pale shadow stripes between black and white stripes
✔ Belly is plain white, sometimes lightly striped near forelegs

 Similar species Hartmann's mountain zebra (alongside) separated by distribution. Plains zebra (p.55) has stripes across the entire belly.

NOTE This is one of two subspecies of mountain zebra. The other is Hartmann's mountain zebra.

AT A GLANCE

✔ Distribution
✔ Lacks pale shadow stripes between black and white stripes
✔ Belly is plain white, sometimes lightly striped near forelegs

 Similar species Cape mountain zebra (alongside) separated by distribution. Plains zebra (p.55) has stripes across the entire belly.

NOTE This is one of two subspecies of mountain zebra. The other is the Cape mountain zebra.

Dogs, foxes, jackals and hyaenas

Members of this diverse group typically have dog-like features, although a hyaena's hind legs are relatively shorter than those of a dog.

Wild dogs and spotted hyaenas are known for their hunting skills, but jackals and foxes are equally capable hunters. The members of this family are largely, but not always strictly, nocturnal. The bat-eared fox and wild dog are exceptions, but the latter does occasionally hunt at night.

The only identification challenges posed by this family lie in distinguishing the jackals from one another and from the Cape fox.

LOOK FOR

- ✔ **fur length**
- ✔ **ear shape**
- ✔ **leg colour and markings**
- ✔ **tail thickness and markings**
- ✔ **side markings**
- ✔ **back colour and markings**

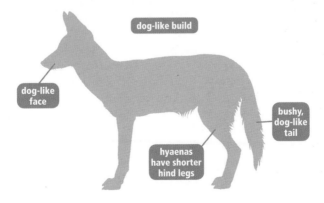

Wild dogs are the rarest members of this visual group.

DOGS, FOXES, JACKALS AND HYAENAS HAVE ONLY ONE VISUAL GROUP

dog-like build

dog-like face

bushy, dog-like tail

hyaenas have shorter hind legs

Wild dog
Wildehond
Lycaon pictus

- large, round ears
- thin, dog-like legs
- blotchy black, white and brown fur

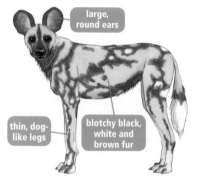

Height 75cm **Weight** 27kg
Habitat Favours open habitat, from grassland and savanna to sparse woodland.
Habits Largely diurnal. Usually in medium-sized to large packs that hunt co-operatively.

✔ Thin, dog-like legs
✔ Large, round ears
✔ Blotchy black, white and brown fur

Similar species None. The large ears and patchy colouring are distinctive.

Spotted hyaena
Gevlekte hiëna
Crocuta crocuta

- pale brown fur with black spots
- dark spots on pale legs
- shorter, more powerful hind legs

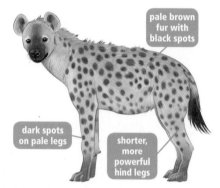

Height 85cm **Weight** 65kg
Habitat A wide range of habitats, including desert, grassland, woodland and even forest.
Habits Predominantly nocturnal, but is often also seen during the day. Family groups vary in size.

✔ Dark spots on pale legs
✔ Pale brown fur with black spots
✔ Shorter, more powerful hind legs

Similar species None. The combination of a typical hyaena's build and small dark spots on pale fur is distinctive.

Brown hyaena
Bruin hiëna
Hyaena brunnea

long, plain, dark fur

pale bands on legs

shorter, more powerful hind legs

Height 80cm **Weight** 42kg
Habitat Ranges widely from desert to woodland, but avoids dense habitat.
Habits Predominantly nocturnal. Often in family groups, but lone males may be encountered.

Aardwolf
Aardwolf
Proteles cristata

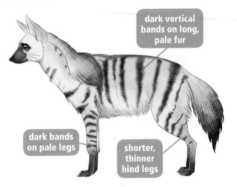

dark vertical bands on long, pale fur

dark bands on pale legs

shorter, thinner hind legs

Height 50cm **Weight** 8kg
Habitat Wide ranging, but absent from desert and forest.
Habits Predominantly nocturnal in summer, but is sometimes seen during the day in winter. Solitary or in pairs.

AT A GLANCE

✔ Pale bands on legs
✔ Long, plain, dark fur
✔ Shorter, more powerful hind legs

 Similar species None. The dark brown coat and banded legs are distinctive.

AT A GLANCE

✔ Dark bands on pale legs
✔ Dark vertical bands on long, pale fur
✔ Shorter, thinner hind legs

 Similar species None. The pale coat with dark bands on both body and legs is quite distinctive.

Bat-eared fox
Bakoorvos
Otocyon megalotis

uniform or graduated back and sides

legs thin, plain and darker than body

outer two-thirds of tail black and bushy

Height 30cm **Weight** 4kg
Habitat Favours open grassland and sparse woodland.
Habits Typically diurnal in winter and nocturnal in summer. Often in pairs or small family groups.

AT A GLANCE
✔ Legs thin, plain and darker than body
✔ Uniform or graduated back and sides
✔ Outer two-thirds of tail black and bushy

 Similar species None. The very large ears, contrasting dark legs and bushy black fur on outer two-thirds of the tail are distinctive.

Cape fox
Silwervos
Vulpes chama

 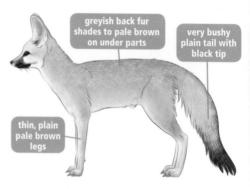

greyish back fur shades to pale brown on under parts

very bushy plain tail with black tip

thin, plain pale brown legs

Height 30cm **Weight** 3kg
Habitat Dry habitats, ranging from grassland and savanna to karoo scrub.
Habits Predominantly nocturnal. Often solitary, but sometimes in pairs.

AT A GLANCE
✔ Thin, plain pale brown legs
✔ Greyish back fur shades to pale brown on under parts
✔ Very bushy plain tail with black tip

 Similar species Jackals (opposite) bear a superficial resemblance, but have less bushy tails and less grey on their backs.

Black-backed jackal
Rooijakkals
Canis mesomelas

Side-striped jackal
Witkwasjakkals
Canis adustus

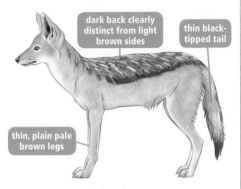

dark back clearly distinct from light brown sides

thin black-tipped tail

thin, plain pale brown legs

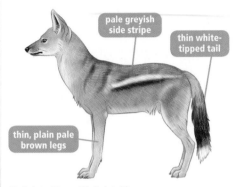

pale greyish side stripe

thin white-tipped tail

thin, plain pale brown legs

Height 40cm **Weight** 8kg
Habitat Ranges widely, from woodland and grassland to very arid areas. Doesn't require drinking water. May venture into rural human settlements.
Habits Usually active at dawn and dusk, but may be seen at any time. Often solitary, but sometimes in small family groups.

Height 40cm **Weight** 8kg
Habitat Typically woodland, but sometimes also in grassy areas.
Habits Usually nocturnal. Often solitary or in small family groups.

AT A GLANCE
✔ Thin, plain pale brown legs
✔ Dark back clearly distinct from light brown sides
✔ Thin black-tipped tail

Similar species Side-striped jackal (alongside) has white-tipped tail. Cape fox (opposite) has much bushier tail and greyer back.

AT A GLANCE
✔ Thin, plain pale brown legs
✔ Pale greyish side stripe
✔ Thin white-tipped tail

Similar species Black-backed jackal (alongside) has black-tipped tail. Cape fox (opposite) has much bushier tail and greyer back.

STEP TWO

Cats

Cats are easily recognised by the distinctive shape of their faces and bodies and by their long, animated tails. All cats other than cheetahs have retractable claws. They are proficient hunters, although scavenged food may make up a minor part of their diet, particularly in the case of the larger cats, which poach prey from smaller ones given the chance.

Most species in this family are quite simple to identify, but pay attention to the pattern of spots to help you distinguish between leopards, cheetahs and servals. Most cat species are nocturnal, although cheetahs hunt by day.

LOOK FOR

✔ **tail length and thickness**
✔ **coat colour and markings**
✔ **ear length**
✔ **size**

Lionesses feeding at a kill.

CATS HAVE ONLY ONE VISUAL GROUP

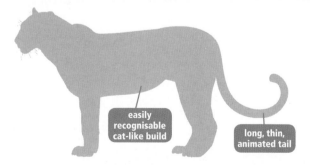

easily recognisable cat-like build

long, thin, animated tail

Lion (female and subadult male)

Leeu

Panthera leo

long, thin, cat-like tail with dark bushy tip

very large size

plain tan fur

Lion (adult male)

Leeu

Panthera leo

iconic and unmistakable

Height 90cm
Weight female, 130kg; subadult male, ±150kg
Habitat Most habitats, but absent from desert and very densely vegetated areas.
Habits Predominantly nocturnal, but may be active at any time of day. Lion prides consist of a dominant male, females and their young, and subadult males. Mature males ejected from prides are usually solitary, but may form small bachelor groups.

Height 1.2m **Weight** 200kg
Habitat Most habitats, but avoids desert and very densely vegetated areas.
Habits Predominantly nocturnal, but may be active at any time of day. Usually in prides comprising a dominant male, females and subadult males.

KF

GK

AT A GLANCE

✔ Very large size
✔ Long, thin, cat-like tail with dark bushy tip
✔ Plain tan fur

Similar-looking species None. Size differentiates it from the caracal (p.66), which is the only other cat in the region with a plain coat. The caracal also has long, pointed ears with hairy black tips.

AT A GLANCE

✔ Iconic and unmistakable

Similar-looking species None. Body size and mane are highly distinctive.

Leopard

Luiperd
Panthera pardus

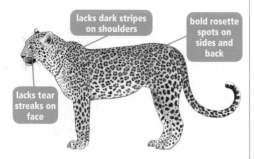

lacks dark stripes on shoulders

bold rosette spots on sides and back

lacks tear streaks on face

Height 75cm **Weight** 50kg
Habitat Wide ranging, including rocky hills, forest and woodland habitat. Avoids exposed habitat as it requires cover.
Habits Predominantly nocturnal, although may be active at any time of day. Usually solitary, but sometimes in pairs.

AT A GLANCE

✔ Lacks tear streaks on face
✔ Lacks dark stripes on shoulders
✔ Bold rosette spots on sides and back

 Similar-looking species Cheetah (alongside) bears a superficial resemblance, but has smaller, solid spots, not rosettes. Leopard may also have some solid spots, but these are confined to the head, chest and lower limbs; its build is bulkier and it lacks tear streaks on the face.

NOTE Leopards can vary enormously in size, but are generally smaller than lions and cheetahs and larger than the remaining cats in this group.

Cheetah

Jagluiperd
Acinonyx jubatus

no dark stripes on shoulders

long, bold tear streaks

solid black spots on pale tan coat

Height 85cm **Weight** 55kg
Habitat Open grassy habitats where it can sprint. Avoids woodland and scrubby areas.
Habits Predominantly diurnal. Usually solitary, but sometimes in mating pairs or small family groups.

AT A GLANCE

✔ Long, bold tear streaks
✔ No dark stripes on shoulders
✔ Solid black spots on pale tan coat

 Similar-looking species Leopard (alongside) bears a superficial resemblance but has black spots with dark tan centres that distinguish it from all other spotted cats. Serval (p.65) has black stripes on the shoulders and large ears with striking white patches. All other spotted cats are far smaller.

NOTE The king cheetah is a rare form of cheetah that does have black stripes on the shoulders. However, its size and the absence of white patches on its ears distinguish it from the serval.

Serval
Tierboskat
Leptailurus serval

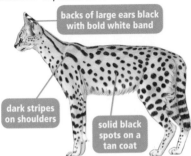

backs of large ears black with bold white band

dark stripes on shoulders

solid black spots on a tan coat

Height 60cm **Weight** 10kg
Habitat Reed beds or flooded grassland, never far from water.
Habits Predominantly nocturnal. Often solitary or in breeding pairs.

Black-footed (small spotted) cat
Klein gekolde kat
Felis nigripes

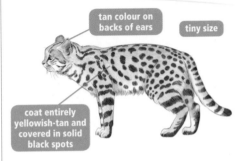

tan colour on backs of ears

tiny size

coat entirely yellowish-tan and covered in solid black spots

Height 23cm **Weight** 1.9kg
Habitat Open dry grassland and scrub.
Habits Predominantly nocturnal. Usually solitary or in breeding pairs.

AT A GLANCE
- ✔ Dark stripes on shoulders
- ✔ Backs of large ears black with bold white band
- ✔ Solid black spots on a tan coat

Similar-looking species Cheetah (p.64) has no black stripes on the shoulders and its ears are shorter, more rounded and lack the white patch. Leopard (p.64) has solid spots only on the head, chest and lower limbs, not the entire coat. King cheetah (p.64) – a mutation of the cheetah – has black shoulder stripes, but is far larger and lacks white bands on its ears.

AT A GLANCE
- ✔ Coat entirely yellowish-tan and covered in solid black spots
- ✔ Tan colour on backs of ears
- ✔ Tiny size

Similar-looking species Genets (p.67) are superficially similar, but more dog-like – they lack the typical facial features of a cat. The black-footed cat is dramatically smaller than any other spotted cat in the region.

Caracal
Rooikat
Caracal caracal

long, pointed ears with hairy black tips

medium size

plain reddish-tan coat

Height 43cm **Weight** 12kg
Habitat Most habitats, but absent from very arid regions.
Habits Predominantly nocturnal. Usually solitary or in breeding pairs.

AT A GLANCE

✔ Medium size
✔ Long, pointed ears with hairy black tips
✔ Plain reddish-tan coat

 Similar-looking species None. Pointed ears with black tufts are distinctive. Female lion (p.63) also has plain coat, but is far larger.

Southern African wildcat
Vaalboskat
Felis silvestris caffra

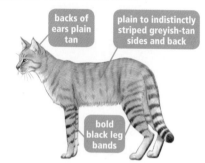

backs of ears plain tan

plain to indistinctly striped greyish-tan sides and back

bold black leg bands

Height 35cm **Weight** 4.5kg
Habitat All but the most arid habitats.
Habits Nocturnal. Usually solitary or in breeding pairs.

AT A GLANCE

✔ Backs of ears plain tan
✔ Plain to indistinctly striped greyish-tan sides and back
✔ Bold black leg bands

 Similar-looking species Although this is the only small striped wildcat in the region, it could be confused with a domestic cat.

NOTE *Felis silvestris caffra* is one of several subspecies of the wildcat.

STEP TWO

Genets and civets

Because they are small and spotted, genets look superficially similar to black-footed cats. However, their pointed snouts and large round ears distinguish them.

The two genets look quite similar, but can be separated by their tail tip colour. The African civet is unique in this group. It has a distinctive rather dog-like build and striking dark legs.

All members of this group are quite strictly nocturnal and are usually solitary.

> ## 👀 LOOK FOR
>
> ✔ **tail markings**
> ✔ **tail tip colour**
> ✔ **leg length**
> ✔ **fur colour**

ND /IOA

The African civet occurs in dense habitat.

GENETS AND CIVETS HAVE ONLY ONE VISUAL GROUP

- **large, rounded ears**
- **pale fur with small black spots**
- **long, thick, banded tail**
- **pointed snout**
- **small size**

Tree (palm) civet
Boomsiwet
Nandinia binotata

 ## African civet
Afrikaanse siwet
Civettictis civetta

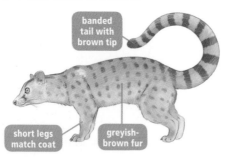

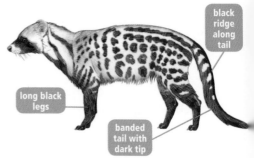

Length 95cm **Weight** 2kg
Habitat Damp montane forest.
Habits Nocturnal. Usually solitary.

Length 1.3m **Weight** 12kg
Habitat Dense woodland and forest.
Habits Nocturnal. Solitary or in small
family groups.

Tree civets occur in montane forest.

AT A GLANCE

✔ Short legs match coat
✔ Banded tail with brown tip
✔ Greyish-brown fur

 Similar-looking species None.
May bear slight resemblance to
the genets (opposite), but has very
restricted range and its greyish-
brown fur and banded brown-
tipped tail are distinctive.

AT A GLANCE

✔ Long black legs
✔ Black ridge along tail
✔ Banded tail with dark tip

 Similar-looking species None
within this group.The long legs
and bushy tail are distinctive. May
superficially resemble a black-
footed cat (p.66), but typically has
more dog-like features.

Small-spotted genet
Kleinkolmuskejaatkat
Genetta genetta

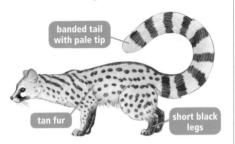

banded tail with pale tip

tan fur

short black legs

Length 95cm **Weight** 2kg
Habitat Varied. Includes woodland, scrub and more arid vegetation. Requires drinking water.
Habits Predominantly nocturnal. Often solitary, but also in small family groups.

AT A GLANCE

✔ Tan fur
✔ Banded tail with pale tip
✔ Short black legs

 Similar-looking species Bears some resemblance to the South African large-spotted genet (alongside), but separated from this and all other species in the group by its pale-tipped tail.

South African large-spotted (rusty-spotted) genet
Rooikolmuskejaatkat
Genetta tigrina

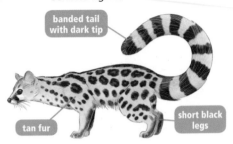

banded tail with dark tip

tan fur

short black legs

Length 1m **Weight** 1.9kg
Habitat Dense vegetation, particularly damp forest. Requires drinking water.
Habits Predominantly nocturnal and largely solitary.

MR / VWC

LBR / VWC

AT A GLANCE

✔ Tan fur
✔ Banded tail with dark tip
✔ Short black legs

Similar-looking species Small-spotted genet (alongside) has white-tipped tail.

STEP TWO

Pigs and hogs

The members of this family resemble typical domestic pigs, making them fairly simple to identify. Warthogs are diurnal, while bushpigs are nocturnal. Both species tend to live in small family groups.

The warthog is the best-known member of this group, because it is active in open areas. The bushpig is secretive and nocturnal and therefore more difficult to locate. However, when encountered, it is quite easy to recognise.

LOOK FOR

✓ **Length and extent of body hair**

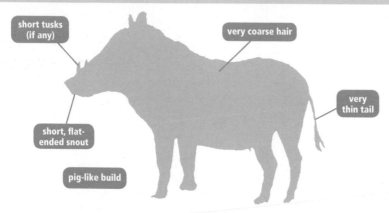

A common warthog at rest, surrounded by its young.

PIGS AND HOGS HAVE ONLY ONE VISUAL GROUP

short tusks
(if any)

very coarse hair

very
thin tail

short, flat-
ended snout

pig-like build

Common warthog
Vlakvark
Phacochoerus africanus

 ## Bushpig
Bosvark
Potamochoerus larvatus

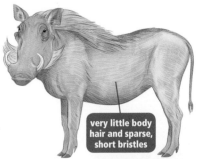

> very little body hair and sparse, short bristles

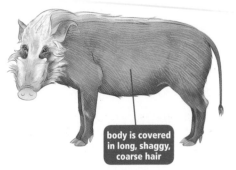

> body is covered in long, shaggy, coarse hair

Height 65cm
Weight 70kg
Habitat Open grassy areas in a wide range of habitats, from woodland to grassland. Often associated with water.
Habits Usually in family groups led by a dominant male. Young males may form bachelor groups.

Height 75cm **Weight** 60kg
Habitat Requires good cover, such as long grass, reed beds or riverine bush. May venture into forest. Always closely associated with water.
Habits Predominantly nocturnal. Usually in family groups (called sounders) led by a dominant male. Young males form bachelor groups.

AT A GLANCE

✔ Very little body hair and sparse, short bristles

Similar species None. Its very short body hair separates it from the bushpig (alongside).

AT A GLANCE

✔ Body is covered in long, shaggy, coarse hair

Similar species None. The long, shaggy coat is distinctive within this group.

Dassies (hyraxes)

Dassies or hyraxes are familiar to many outdoor enthusiasts. All dassies look rather like oversized hamsters, but you can tell them apart by paying careful attention to the colour of the spot on the back, the colour of the face relative to the body, and the prominence of the eyebrows.

Because dassies are the ideal prey for a wide range of predators, they remain close to shelter and have evolved both a fairly complex communication system and a social hierarchy organised to help them identify and respond rapidly to danger.

🔭 LOOK FOR

- ✔ belly colour
- ✔ back spot colour
- ✔ face colour
- ✔ prominence of eyebrows
- ✔ eye patches

Rock dassies like those shown here may fall prey to raptors, leopards and jackals, among others.

HYRAXES HAVE ONLY ONE VISUAL GROUP

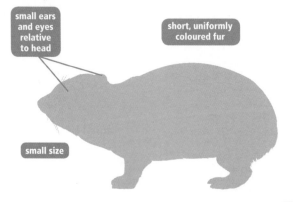

small ears and eyes relative to head

short, uniformly coloured fur

small size

Rock dassie (hyrax)
Klipdas
Procavia capensis

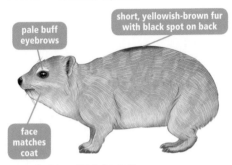

pale buff eyebrows

short, yellowish-brown fur with black spot on back

face matches coat

Length 50cm **Weight** 3.5kg
Habitat Ranges widely, but favours rocky outcrops and coastal scrub.
Habits Diurnal. In fairly large family groups.

AT A GLANCE

✔ Face matches coat
✔ Pale buff eyebrows
✔ Short, yellowish-brown fur with black spot on back

 Similar species Superficially resembles other dassies, but distinguished by black spot on its back.

Kaokoveld rock dassie (hyrax)
Kaokoveldklipdas
Procavia capensis welwitschii

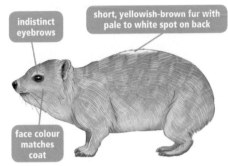

indistinct eyebrows

short, yellowish-brown fur with pale to white spot on back

face colour matches coat

Length 50cm **Weight** 3.5kg
Habitat Ranges widely, but favours rocky outcrops in dry areas.
Habits Predominantly diurnal. In fairly large family groups.

Rocky outcrops in dry regions provide ideal habitat for Kaokoveld dassies.

AT A GLANCE

✔ Face colour matches coat
✔ Indistinct eyebrows
✔ Short, yellowish-brown fur with pale to white spot on back

 Similar species Tree and yellow-spotted (p.74) dassies have striking facial markings. Rock dassie (alongside) has black spot on its back.

Tree dassie (hyrax)
Boomdas
Dendrohyrax arboreus

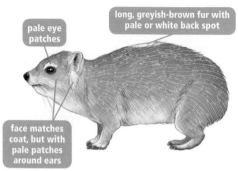

pale eye patches

long, greyish-brown fur with pale or white back spot

face matches coat, but with pale patches around ears

Length 52cm **Weight** 2.3kg
Habitat Dwells in trees and favours forested habitat.
Habits Diurnal. Usually solitary, but sometimes in pairs.

HS / WC

AT A GLANCE
✔ Face matches coat, but with pale patches around ears
✔ Pale eye patches
✔ Long, greyish-brown fur with pale or white back spot

 Similar species Yellow-spotted dassie's (alongside) face is markedly paler than its body, with striking white eyebrows. Kaokoveld dassie (p.73) has indistinct eyebrows and its face colour matches its coat. Rock dassie (p.73) has black spot on its back.

 ## Yellow-spotted dassie (hyrax)
Geelkoldassie
Heterohyrax brucei

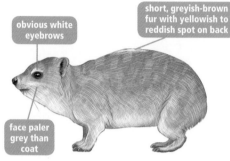

obvious white eyebrows

short, greyish-brown fur with yellowish to reddish spot on back

face paler grey than coat

Length 35cm **Weight** 2.5kg
Habitat Rocky slopes and hills.
Habits Diurnal. In small to medium-sized family groups.

DN

AT A GLANCE
✔ Face paler grey than coat
✔ Obvious white eyebrows
✔ Short, greyish-brown fur with yellowish to reddish spot on back

 Similar species Tree dassie (alongside) has pale patches around ears and eyes. Kaokoveld dassie (p.73) has indistinct eyebrows and its face colour matches its coat. Rock dassie (p.73) has a black spot on its back.

SEPARATING VISUAL GROUPS

Rabbits and hares

Rabbits and hares have a distinctive shape, characteristic long ears and large eyes – adaptations that suit their nocturnal lifestyle. All except for the springhare have short tails. They hop using their powerful hind legs and are often solitary.

In a chase, rabbits and hares flee in a straight line, and then dart off to one side just as the predator is ready to pounce. This habit of running straight has led to the mistaken belief that a rabbit can be caught in a vehicle's headlights.

The nuchal patch is an important feature in the identification of rabbits and hares. This is a patch of fur on the back of the neck that differs in colour from the rest of the body. It is not always easy to see.

LB / WVC

Note this scrub hare's white tail, a characteristic that distinguishes hares from rabbits.

LOOK FOR

- ✔ tail length
- ✔ tail markings and colour
- ✔ face and jawline markings and colour
- ✔ nuchal patch colour

RABBITS AND HARES HAVE ONLY ONE VISUAL GROUP

long ears (except for springhare) and large eyes relative to head

short, uniformly coloured fur

small size

tail short and bushy, but long in springhare

Riverine rabbit
Rivierkonyn
Bunolagus monticularis

rufous nuchal patch

greyish tail

striking black-and-white jawline markings

Length 50cm **Weight** 1.7kg
Habitat Restricted to riverine habitats, as its common names suggest.
Habits Nocturnal. Almost always solitary.

AT A GLANCE

✔ Striking black-and-white jawline markings
✔ Rufous nuchal patch
✔ Greyish tail

Similar-looking species Natal red rock rabbit (p.78) has an obvious jawline that lacks the black. All other rabbits and hares have plainer faces. Hares have white on their tails.

Springhare
Springhaas
Pedetes capensis

very long tail with black tip

Length 80cm **Weight** 3kg
Habitat Favours sandy habitat. Absent only from arid areas.
Habits Nocturnal. Very seldom seen by day. Usually in burrows with several family members.

AT A GLANCE

✔ Very long tail with black tip

Similar-looking species None. The long, black-tipped tail is unique in this group. Note also the short arms, relatively short ears and very long hind feet.

Scrub hare
Kolhaas
Lepus saxatilis

Cape hare
Vlakhaas
Lepus capensis

tail black above, white below

white belly

short tail

tail black above, white below

belly buff or white with buff patches

short tail

Length 50cm **Weight** 3kg
Habitat Wide ranging, including woodland and scrub. Avoids exposed and very arid areas.
Habits Predominantly nocturnal. Usually solitary.

Length 60cm **Weight** 2kg
Habitat Grassland, patchy scrub and even desert.
Habits Predominantly nocturnal. Usually solitary or in small family groups.

AT A GLANCE

✔ White belly
✔ Tail black above, white below
✔ Short tail

Similar-looking species Cape hare (alongside) has buff belly or buff belly patches. Unlike rabbits, hares have white on their tails.

AT A GLANCE

✔ Belly buff or white with buff patches
✔ Tail black above, white below
✔ Short tail

Similar-looking species Scrub hare (alongside) has entirely white belly. Unlike rabbits, hares have white on their tails.

Jameson's red rock rabbit
Jameson se rooiklipkonyn
Pronolagus randensis

greyish head with brown flecking; no prominent jawline markings

rump and hind legs paler than body

Length 55cm **Weight** 2.5kg
Habitat Rocky, hilly areas throughout its range. Requires crevices in which to rest by day.
Habits Nocturnal. Seen during the day only when flushed from its resting place. Usually solitary, but sometimes in small family groups.

Jameson's red rock rabbit requires rocky habitat with crevices in which to shelter.

AT A GLANCE

✔ Distribution
✔ Greyish head with brown flecking; no prominent jawline markings
✔ Rump and hind legs paler than body

Similar-looking species Jameson's, Smith's and Hewitt's red rock rabbits (opposite) are indistinguishable in the field and are best separated on distribution (although there is some overlap in the Free State). Natal red rock rabbit (alongside) has a prominent white jawline.

Natal red rock rabbit
Natalse rooiklipkonyn
Pronolagus crassicaudatus

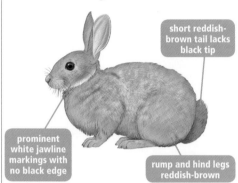

short reddish-brown tail lacks black tip

prominent white jawline markings with no black edge

rump and hind legs reddish-brown

Length 55cm **Weight** 2.5kg
Habitat Rocky, hilly areas throughout its range. Requires crevices in which to rest by day.
Habits Nocturnal. Seen during the day only when flushed from its resting place. Usually solitary, but sometimes in small family groups.

These rocky slopes in KwaZulu-Natal are good habitat for the Natal red rock rabbit.

AT A GLANCE

✔ Prominent white jawline markings with no black edge
✔ Short, reddish-brown tail lacks black tip
✔ Rump and hind legs reddish-brown

Similar-looking species Separated from Jameson's (alongside), Smith's and Hewitt's red rock rabbits (opposite) by its prominent white jawline.

Smith's and Hewitt's red rock rabbits

Smith se rooiklipkonyn,
Hewitt se rooiklipkonyn
Pronolagus rupestris,
Pronolagus saundersiae

sides of face greyish; no prominent jawline markings

rump and hind legs reddish-brown

Length 55cm **Weight** 1.5kg
Habitat Rocky, hilly areas throughout its range. Requires crevices in which to rest by day.
Habits Nocturnal. Seen during the day only when flushed from its resting place. Usually solitary, but sometimes in small family groups.

Smith's red rock rabbit favours rocky areas in the Western Cape.

AT A GLANCE

✔ Distribution
✔ Sides of face greyish; no prominent jawline markings
✔ Rump and hind legs reddish-brown

Similar-looking species Jameson's (opposite), Smith's and Hewitt's red rock rabbits are indistinguishable in the field and are best separated on distribution (although their ranges overlap slightly in the Free State). Natal red rock rabbit (opposite) has a prominent white jawline.

Hewitt's red rock rabbit (alongside) inhabits rocky areas in the Western Cape.

Scrub vegetation is the favoured habitat of both scrub and Cape hares (p.77).

Squirrels

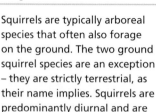

Squirrels are typically arboreal species that often also forage on the ground. The two ground squirrel species are an exception – they are strictly terrestrial, as their name implies. Squirrels are predominantly diurnal and are usually solitary, although they may occur in pairs.

Their chubby-cheeked faces and the shape of their bushy tails make them readily identifiable. Some members of this family actually have thin tails, but they still exhibit a typical squirrel's tail shape.

The ground squirrel species are most difficult to separate, as the only way to tell them apart is by counting the number of black bands on a single tail hair.

NOTE The grey squirrel – a species introduced from Europe – is included in this visual group.

The South African ground squirrel is a strictly terrestrial species.

LOOK FOR

✔ tail markings and colours
✔ tail thickness
✔ flank markings and colours
✔ leg and jaw colour
✔ distribution

SQUIRRELS HAVE ONLY ONE VISUAL GROUP

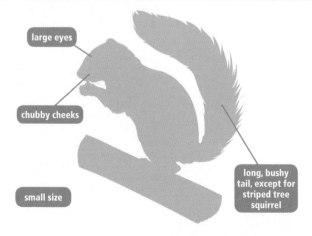

large eyes

chubby cheeks

small size

long, bushy tail, except for striped tree squirrel

South African ground squirrel
Waaistertgrondeekhoring
Xerus inauris

Mutable sun squirrel
Soneekhoring
Heliosciurus mutabilis

bushy black-and-white streaked tail

two black bands on each tail hair (see NOTE below)

single white flank streak

tail has dark and light brown bands

Length 45cm **Weight** 630g
Habitat Open grassy habitat with low bush.
Habits Largely diurnal. In medium-sized to large groups, comprising females and their young, led by a dominant male.

Length 52cm **Weight** 390g
Habitat Evergreen forest. Typically seen near the crown of a tree.
Habits Largely diurnal. Usually solitary or in pairs, but sometimes with young.

Mutable sun squirrels occur in evergreen forests. Look for them in the crown of a tree.

AT A GLANCE

✔ Single white flank streak
✔ Bushy black-and-white streaked tail
✔ Two black bands on each tail hair

Similar-looking species
Superficially resembles the striped tree squirrel (p.82), but that species is distinguished by its long, plain tail. All other squirrels lack an obvious flank streak.

NOTE The Damara (mountain) squirrel *Xerus princeps* is almost identical, but has three black bands on each tail hair. Although their ideal habitat differs, these species do overlap in some areas.

AT A GLANCE

✔ Tail has dark and light brown bands

Similar-looking species None. The banded tail is diagnostic.

Striped tree squirrel

Gestreepte boomeekhoring
Funisciurus congicus

thin tail

long, plain-coloured tail

white flank streak with black borders

Length 32cm **Weight** 110g
Habitat Dense woodland. Requires drinking water in its habitat.
Habits Largely diurnal. Usually solitary or in small groups.

AT A GLANCE

✔ Thin tail
✔ Long, plain-coloured tail
✔ White flank streak with black borders

Similar-looking species Both ground squirrels (p.81) superficially resemble striped tree squirrel, but have bushier, streaked tails. All other squirrels lack the obvious white flank streak.

Tree squirrel

Boomeekhoring
Paraxerus cepapi

plain-coloured tail

uniformly coloured upper parts, legs and lower jaw

Length 37cm **Weight** 175g
Habitat Open savanna and woodland.
Habits Largely diurnal. Usually in pairs or accompanied by young.

AT A GLANCE

✔ Distribution
✔ Uniformly coloured upper parts, legs and lower jaw
✔ Plain-coloured tail

Similar-looking species Best told from grey squirrel (opposite) on distribution. Red bush squirrel's (opposite) legs, tail and jaw contrast with its body colour. Mutable sun squirrel (p.81) has distinct bands on its tail. The ground (p.81) and striped tree (alongside) squirrels have an obvious white flank streak.

Grey squirrel
Gryseekhoring
Sciurus carolinensis

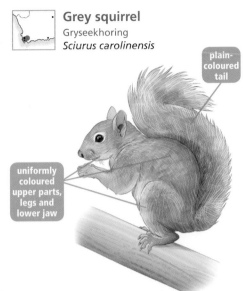

plain-coloured tail

uniformly coloured upper parts, legs and lower jaw

Red bush squirrel
Rooi eekhoring
Paraxerus palliatus

plain-coloured tail

reddish to yellowish legs, tail and lower jaw contrast with body colour

plain-coloured upper parts

Length 40cm **Weight** 300g
Habitat Thick bush in forest and woodland. Stays close to the ground.
Habits Largely diurnal. Often in pairs, sometimes with young.

Length 40cm **Weight** 500g
Habitat Introduced from Europe and readily seen in parks and gardens in Cape Town.
Habits Largely diurnal. Usually solitary, but sometimes in pairs or with young.

D / WC

AVZ / IOA

AT A GLANCE

✔ Distribution
✔ Uniformly coloured upper parts, legs and lower jaw
✔ Plain-coloured tail

 Similar-looking species Tree squirrel (opposite) is best separated on distribution. Red bush squirrel's (alongside) legs, tail and jaw contrast with its body colour; also separated on distribution. Mutable sun squirrel (p.81) has banded tail. The ground (p.81) and striped tree (opposite) squirrels have an obvious white flank streak.

AT A GLANCE

✔ Reddish to yellowish legs, tail and lower jaw contrast with body colour
✔ Plain-coloured tail
✔ Plain-coloured upper parts

 Similar-looking species In tree (opposite) and grey (alongside) squirrels there is no contrast between body colour and leg, tail and jaw colour. Grey squirrel also has different distribution. Mutable sun squirrel (p.81) has banded tail. The ground (p.81) and striped tree squirrels (opposite) have an obvious white flank streak.

SEPARATING VISUAL GROUPS

Mongooses and suricate

Mongooses and their relative the suricate have elongated bodies and long tails. Their legs are usually short, but a few have long legs and may look almost dog-like. Typically, mongooses have a small head, short snout and beady eyes.

They are ground-dwellers and tend to remain under cover, but occasionally dart across open areas. Many mongoose species can stand upright on their hind legs to look out for predators and prey. The water mongoose is an unusual member of the group in that it is the only mongoose in the region that is adapted for life in and around water.

Members of this group are usually solitary, but some live in small family groups.

 LOOK FOR

✔ coat colour
✔ tail markings, colour and thickness
✔ nose colour
✔ fur length
✔ back markings
✔ leg length and colour

S and J / WC

Suricates are best known for their upright 'lookout' stance.

MONGOOSES AND SURICATE CAN BE DIVIDED INTO TWO VISUAL GROUPS

Boldly banded back (go to p.85)

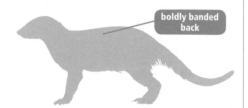

boldly banded back

Plain or indistinctly banded back (go to p.86)

plain or indistinctly banded back

Suricate (meerkat)
Stokstertmeerkat
Suricata suricatta

Banded mongoose
Gebande muishond
Mungos mungo

pale yellow coat

dark bands on back

yellowish tail with black tip

greyish-brown coat

dark bands on back

plain grey tail

Length 50cm **Weight** 750g
Habitat Varied. Includes arid karoo, woodland and grassland. Favours flat ground.
Habits Diurnal. Lives in family groups in a burrow system.

Length 60cm **Weight** 1.4kg
Habitat Woodland.
Habits Active mainly during the day. In small to large packs comprising females and their young, led by a dominant male.

AT A GLANCE

✔ Pale yellow coat
✔ Dark bands on back
✔ Yellowish tail with black tip

Similar-looking species None. The yellowish coat is distinctive.

AT A GLANCE

✔ Greyish-brown coat
✔ Dark bands on back
✔ Plain grey tail

Similar-looking species None. The only member of this visual group that has a greyish-brown coat.

Meller's mongoose
Meller se muishond
Rhynchogale melleri

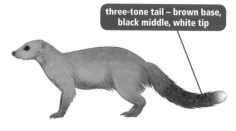

three-tone tail – brown base, black middle, white tip

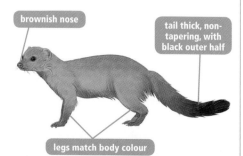

brownish nose

tail thick, non-tapering, with black outer half

legs match body colour

Length 85cm **Weight** 2.5kg
Habitat Woodland and grassland.
Habits Nocturnal. Usually solitary, but females may be accompanied by their young.

AT A GLANCE

Form with white-tipped tail
✔ Three-tone tail – brown base, black middle, white tip

Form with black-tipped tail
✔ Brownish nose
✔ Tail thick, non-tapering, with black outer half
✔ Legs match body colour

Similar-looking species The white-tipped form is separated from all other mongooses by its tail markings. The black-tipped form is separated from all other mongooses by its tail shape and the extensive black on the outer half of its tail.

Dwarf mongoose
Dwergmuishond
Helogale parvula

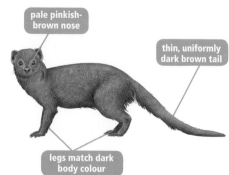

pale pinkish-brown nose

thin, uniformly dark brown tail

legs match dark body colour

Length 40cm **Weight** 270g
Habitat Savanna, but occasionally also ventures into woodland.
Habits Diurnal. In fairly large groups.

AT A GLANCE

✔ Pale pinkish-brown nose
✔ Thin, uniformly dark brown tail
✔ Legs match dark body colour

Similar-looking species None. Its tiny size, dark brown coat and pale pinkish-brown nose are distinctive.

Large grey (Egyptian) mongoose
Groot grysmuishond
Herpestes ichneumon

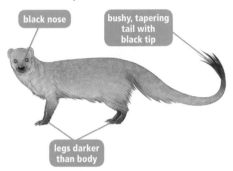

black nose

bushy, tapering tail with black tip

legs darker than body

Length 1m **Weight** 3.3kg
Habitat On the margins of water bodies, particularly in grassland or crop land.
Habits Predominantly diurnal. Usually solitary, although females may be accompanied by their young.

AT A GLANCE
✔ Black nose
✔ Bushy, tapering tail with black tip
✔ Legs darker than body

Similar-looking species Slender mongoose (p.88) also has black tail tip, but has a brown nose and paler legs. One form of Meller's mongoose (opposite) has black on its tail, but this covers the outer half, not just the tip, of the tail. Other members of this group have white-tipped or uniformly coloured tails.

Cape (small) grey mongoose
Klein grysmuishond
Galerella pulverulenta

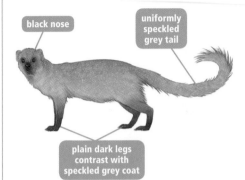

black nose

uniformly speckled grey tail

plain dark legs contrast with speckled grey coat

Length 65cm **Weight** 900g
Habitat Varies widely from karoo to forest, but requires some cover.
Habits Largely diurnal. Usually solitary, but sometimes in small family groups.

AT A GLANCE
✔ Black nose
✔ Uniformly speckled grey tail
✔ Plain dark legs contrast with speckled grey coat

Similar-looking species None. The only mongoose that has a uniformly speckled grey tail.

Slender mongoose
Swartkwasmuishond
Galerella sanguinea

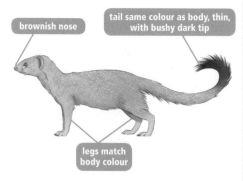

brownish nose

tail same colour as body, thin, with bushy dark tip

legs match body colour

Length 60cm **Weight** 600g
Habitat Wide ranging, including arid areas, grassland and woodland.
Habits Largely diurnal. Usually solitary, but female may be accompanied by young.

AT A GLANCE

✔ Brownish nose
✔ Tail same colour as body, thin, with bushy dark tip
✔ Legs match body colour

 Similar-looking species None. Large grey mongoose (p.87) has black nose and its legs are darker than its body. One form of Meller's mongoose (p.86) has black tail tip, but its tail is much thicker. All other members of this group have either white-tipped or uniformly coloured tails.

Yellow mongoose
Witkwasmuishond
Cynictis penicillata

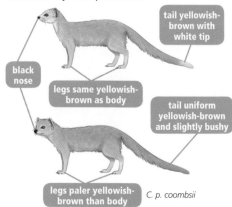

tail yellowish-brown with white tip

black nose

legs same yellowish-brown as body

tail uniform yellowish-brown and slightly bushy

legs paler yellowish-brown than body

C. p. coombsii

Length 55cm **Weight** 600g
Habitat Exposed habitat such as grassland, savanna and arid karoo.
Habits Predominantly diurnal. In colonies of up to 12 animals. Forages alone or in pairs.

AT A GLANCE

All races except C. p. coombsii
✔ Black nose
✔ Tail yellowish-brown with white tip
✔ Legs same yellowish-brown as body

C. p. coombsii race
✔ Black nose
✔ Tail uniform yellowish-brown and slightly bushy
✔ Legs paler yellowish-brown than body

 Similar-looking species Except for *C. p. coombsii*, all races of yellow mongoose have white-tipped tails, lack the darker legs of Selous' (p.90) and white-tailed (opposite) mongooses and lack the black tail ring of Meller's mongoose (p.86). *C. p. coombsii* distinguished from all other mongooses by uniform yellowish-brown tail and legs that are paler than body. Bushy-tailed (opposite), dwarf (p.86) and water (p.90) mongooses all have dark tails and contrasting dark legs.

White-tailed mongoose
Witstertmuishond
Ichneumia albicauda

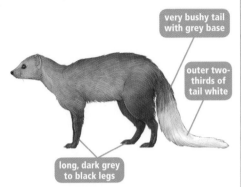

very bushy tail with grey base

outer two-thirds of tail white

long, dark grey to black legs

Length 1m **Weight** 4.3kg
Habitat Savanna and woodland.
Habits Predominantly nocturnal. Usually solitary, but females are sometimes accompanied by young.

AT A GLANCE
✔ Very bushy tail with grey base
✔ Outer two-thirds of tail white
✔ Long, dark grey to black legs

Similar-looking species None. The very bushy white-tipped tail and long black legs are distinctive. No other mongoose has as much white at the end of its tail.

Bushy-tailed mongoose
Borselstertmuishond
Bdeogale crassicauda

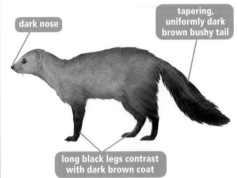

dark nose

tapering, uniformly dark brown bushy tail

long black legs contrast with dark brown coat

Length 70cm **Weight** 1.8kg
Habitat Rocky areas near rivers.
Habits Nocturnal. Usually solitary.

Bushy-tailed mongooses occur in rocky areas close to rivers.

AT A GLANCE
✔ Dark nose
✔ Tapering, uniformly dark brown bushy tail
✔ Long black legs contrast with dark brown coat

Similar-looking species Water mongoose (p.90) has a pink nose and its legs and coat are the same colour. The dwarf mongoose (p.86) is much smaller, with a pale nose and thin tail.

Selous' mongoose
Klein witstertmuishond
Paracynictis selousi

Water (marsh) mongoose
Kommetjiegatmuishond
Atilax paludinosus

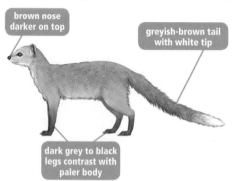

brown nose darker on top

greyish-brown tail with white tip

dark grey to black legs contrast with paler body

pink nose darker on top

uniformly dark brown, bushy, tapering tail

dark legs match dark coat

Length 75cm **Weight** 1.7kg
Habitat Mainly woodland but ventures into scrubby areas.
Habits Predominantly nocturnal. Usually solitary, but females may sometimes be accompanied by young.

Length 90cm **Weight** 3.2kg
Habitat In and around water (both fresh and sea water).
Habits Largely diurnal. Usually solitary, but females may be accompanied by young.

AB / NHPA / Photoshot

AR

AT A GLANCE
✔ Pink nose darker on top
✔ Uniformly dark brown, bushy, tapering tail
✔ Dark legs match dark coat

 Similar-looking species None. The uniformly dark brown, distinctively shaped tail has a very bushy base tapering to a thin point, and is unique within this group.

NOTE The shape of the face (especially when seen in the water) separates this mongoose from otters (opposite), which have far rounder faces and blunt-ended snouts.

AT A GLANCE
✔ Brown nose darker on top
✔ Greyish-brown tail with white tip
✔ Dark grey to black legs contrast with paler body

 Similar-looking species The combination of white tail tip, dark legs contrasting with paler body and two-tone nose is distinctive.

SEPARATING VISUAL GROUPS

Otters

It is a pleasure to observe these apparently playful mammals as they move deftly through water in search of food. The only other water-based mammal with which an otter could be confused is the water mongoose, but otters have short hair and rounder faces.

In theory it isn't difficult to separate the two otter species, since Cape clawless otters are distinctly larger than their spotted-necked relatives and have striking two-tone faces and noticeably paler under parts. In practice, however, it can be tricky to distinguish these key features in the water.

👀 LOOK FOR

✔ **colour of under parts**
✔ **throat markings**
✔ **length**
✔ **size**

Cape clawless otters are far larger than spotted-necked otters.

OTTERS HAVE ONLY ONE VISUAL GROUP

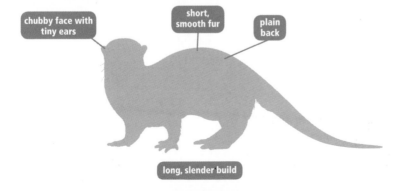

chubby face with tiny ears

short, smooth fur

plain back

long, slender build

Spotted-necked otter
Kleinotter
Lutra maculicollis

small head with dark cheeks

dark under parts

white spots or patches on dark throat

Length 1m **Weight** 4.5kg
Habitat Strictly fresh water, including rivers, lakes, dams and wetlands.
Habits Active mainly during the morning and evening. Often in small family groups.

A pair of spotted-necked otters swimming.

AT A GLANCE

✔ White spots or patches on dark throat
✔ Small head with dark cheeks
✔ Dark under parts

Similar-looking species Cape clawless otter (alongside) is significantly larger with a rounder face and distinctly pale chin, cheeks, chest and belly.

Cape (African) clawless otter
Groototter
Aonyx capensis

large head with pale cheeks

throat lacks spots

pale throat and chest

Length 1.4m **Weight** 15kg
Habitat Fresh water. Also occurs in marine habitats, provided it has access to fresh water.
Habits Active mainly during the morning and evening. Often in small family groups.

AT A GLANCE

✔ Pale throat and chest
✔ Large head with pale cheeks
✔ Throat lacks spots

Similar-looking species Spotted-necked otter (alongside) is significantly smaller, with dark cheeks, thinner face, dark under parts, and white spots and/or patches on its dark throat.

STEP TWO

Badger, polecat and weasel

Although these species are not closely related taxonomically, they are grouped together here because they all have striking black-and-white or silver-grey coats, an elongated build and relatively short legs. These features make the members of this group fairly straightforward to identify.

Although the badger, polecat and weasel are all nocturnal, you may well spot honey badgers during the day. Striped polecats do not run away from danger, but rather turn and spray a foul-smelling fluid at any would-be attacker. This tactic is also employed against vehicles, which is why so many polecats die on the roads.

LOOK FOR

✔ **back markings and colour**
✔ **side markings and colour**
✔ **head markings**
✔ **patches in front of ears**

TC /IOA

Honey badgers are much larger than polecats or weasels.

THE BADGER, POLECAT AND WEASEL HAVE ONLY ONE VISUAL GROUP

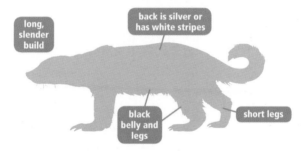

long, slender build

back is silver or has white stripes

black belly and legs

short legs

Honey badger

Ratel
Mellivora capensis

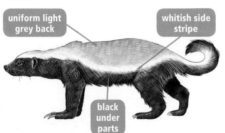

uniform light grey back

whitish side stripe

black under parts

Length 95cm **Weight** 11kg
Habitat Ranges widely and occurs in most grassland, savanna and woodland habitats.
Habits May be active at any time of the day or night, but avoids the midday heat. A nomadic species that is found alone, in pairs or in small groups.

AT A GLANCE

✔ Uniform light grey back
✔ Whitish side stripe
✔ Black under parts

 Similar-looking species None. Its size, pale upper parts and black under parts are distinctive.

Striped polecat

Stinkmuishond
Ictonyx striatus

top of head is dark

white stripes on black back

white patches in front of ears

Length 60cm **Weight** 900g
Habitat Widespread in most habitats.
Habits Strictly nocturnal. Solitary, but sometimes in small family groups. Often killed on the road.

AT A GLANCE

✔ White patches in front of ears
✔ Top of head is dark
✔ White stripes on black back

 Similar-looking species African striped weasel (below) has a slender tail and the top of its head is white.

African striped (white-naped) weasel

Slangmuishond
Poecilogale albinucha

top of head is white

white stripes on black back

dark patches in front of ears

Length 50cm **Weight** 300g
Habitat Damp grassland and woodland.
Habits Strictly nocturnal. Solitary, but sometimes in small family groups.

AT A GLANCE

✔ Dark patches in front of ears
✔ Top of head is white
✔ White stripes on black back

 Similar-looking species Striped polecat (above) has a bushy tail and no white stripes on forehead.

SEPARATING VISUAL GROUPS

Primates

It is usually quite simple to determine whether you are looking at a baboon, monkey or bushbaby (galago), since these primates differ markedly both in size (even the largest bushbaby is dramatically smaller than the tiniest monkey) and behaviour (bushbabies are nocturnal and solitary, while monkeys and baboons are diurnal and social). There are also obvious differences in physical appearance that help to separate species within each of these groups, of which fur colour is often critical.

Vervet monkeys can adapt well to life in a suburban environment.

The chacma baboon is common and widespread. Monkeys are also widespread in southern Africa, but galagos have a far more restricted distribution.

Bushbabies are enigmatic nocturnal creatures that are often encountered in game reserve camps, uttering their strange cries. Small and endearing, they have large forward-facing eyes and long tails. Although their hands and feet are monkey-like, they are so much smaller that confusion is unlikely. The easiest species to identify is the thick-tailed bushbaby, which is the largest, while lesser and Grant's lesser bushbabies are easily separated on the colour of their tail tips.

🔭 LOOK FOR

✔ build
✔ size of eyes and ears
✔ body colour
✔ cheek colour
✔ facial border
✔ limb, hand and foot colour
✔ thickness of tail base
✔ colour of tail tip

PRIMATES CAN BE DIVIDED INTO TWO VISUAL GROUPS

Small eyes; small ears (go to p.96)

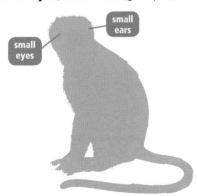

small ears

small eyes

Large eyes; large ears (go to p.98)

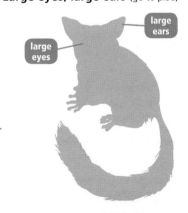

large ears

large eyes

 ## Vervet monkey
Blouaap
Cercopithecus pygerythrus

light build • **striking black face with white border** • **grey arms, hands and feet**

Length 1.2m **Weight** 5kg
Habitat Woodland, savanna, gardens and parks. Requires drinking water and trees in its habitat, but avoids dense forest.
Habits Predominantly diurnal. In small to medium-sized mixed sex troops, led by a dominant male.

GK

AT A GLANCE
✔ Grey arms, hands and feet
✔ Light build
✔ Striking black face with white border

 Similar-looking species Samango monkey (alongside) has striking dark arms, hands and feet and occurs in different habitat.

 ## Samango (Sykes') monkey
Samango-aap
Cercopithecus albogularis

indistinct or no border around dark grey face • **light build** • **striking dark arms, hands and feet**

Length male, 1.4m; female, 1.1m
Weight male, 9.5kg; female, 5kg
Habitat Restricted mainly to forests, but may venture into plantations.
Habits Predominantly diurnal. In small to medium-sized troops, led by a dominant male.

DG and ER / WC

AT A GLANCE
✔ Indistinct or no border around dark grey face
✔ Light build
✔ Striking dark arms, hands and feet

 Similar-looking species Vervet monkey (alongside) has a paler border around its striking black face and occurs in different habitat.

Chacma baboon

Kaapse bobbejaan
Papio hamadryas ursinus

dark cheeks

heavy build

greyish-brown coat

Length male, 1.6m; female, 1.1m
Weight male, 35kg; female, 16kg
Habitat Occurs in most types of habitat, but requires reliable sources of food and water.
Habits Predominantly diurnal. In small to medium-sized family groups, led by a dominant male. May scavenge for food in human settlements.

GK

AT A GLANCE

✔ Dark cheeks
✔ Heavy build
✔ Greyish-brown coat

 Similar-looking species None.

Typical habitats for this visual group

DN

Human settlements regularly encroach on baboon habitat.

DN

Vervet monkeys (opposite) are most at home in well-established woodland.

GK

Samango monkeys (opposite) are found in dense escarpment forest.

Lesser bushbaby (South African galago)
Nagapie
Galago moholi

 ## Grant's lesser bushbaby (Grant's galago)
Grant se nagapie
Galagoides granti

greyish to yellowish fur

base of tail is thin

tail lacks dark tip

brownish fur

base of tail is thin

tail has a dark tip

Length 40cm **Weight** 150g
Habitat Ranges widely from woodland to forest and riverine bush. Always in wooded habitat.
Habits Strictly nocturnal. Solitary or in small family groups.

Length 40cm **Weight** 160g
Habitat Confined almost exclusively to forest.
Habits Strictly nocturnal. Usually solitary or in small family groups.

AT A GLANCE

✔ Tail lacks dark tip
✔ Greyish to yellowish fur
✔ Base of tail is thin

 Similar-looking species Grant's lesser bushbaby (alongside) has browner fur and a dark-tipped tail. Thick-tailed bushbaby (opposite) has a thick, bushy tail base and is far larger.

AT A GLANCE

✔ Tail has a dark tip
✔ Brownish fur
✔ Base of tail is thin

 Similar-looking species Lesser bushbaby (alongside) has greyish to yellowish fur and a uniformly coloured tail that lacks the dark tip. Thick-tailed bushbaby (opposite) has a thick, bushy tail base and is much larger.

Thick-tailed (greater) bushbaby

Bosnagaap

Otolemur crassicaudatus

thick, bushy tail base

Length 75cm **Weight** 1.3kg

Habitat A tree-dwelling species that favours woodland, forest and plantations. Almost always found in tree canopies.

Habits Nocturnal. Solitary, or occurs in small family groups.

AT A GLANCE

✔ Thick, bushy tail base

 Similar-looking species None. This is the only galago with a thick, bushy tail base.

NOTE The tail sometimes has a dark tip, but its thick, bushy base is diagnostic. This species is also 6–10 times heavier than other galagos, and has a very chubby appearance.

Typical habitats for this visual group

Woodland night sounds often include the eerie calls of the lesser bushbaby (opposite).

Thick-tailed bushbabies (alongside) are often seen in rest camps at the Kruger National Park.

Grant's lesser bushbaby (opposite) favours dense forest.

Appendix

In order that similar-looking species could be grouped together for comparative purposes, strict taxonomic sequences have not been adhered to in the 'family' groups described in this book. For those interested in taxonomic relationships, the groupings in this book are represented by the following families and genera. Note that taxonomically distinctive mammals comprise species from a wide range of genera.

Distinctive mammals

Family: Elephantidae
Genus: *Loxodonta* (African elephant)

Family: Erinaceidae
Genus: *Atelerix* (southern African hedgehog)

Family: Giraffidae
Genus: *Giraffa* (giraffe)

Family: Hippopotamidae
Genus: *Hippopotamus* (hippopotamus)

Family: Hystricidae
Genus: *Hystrix* (porcupine)

Family: Manidae
Genus: *Manis* (ground pangolin)

Family: Orycteropodidae
Genus: *Orycteropus* (aardvark)

Family: Rhinocerotidae
Genera: *Ceratotherium* (white rhino),
Diceros (black rhino)

Giraffes

Antelope and buffalo

Family: Bovidae
Genera: *Aepyceros* (impala/black-faced impala), *Alcelaphus* (Lichtenstein's hartebeest, red hartebeest), *Antidorcas* (springbok), *Cephalophus* (red duiker), *Connochaetes* (black wildebeest, blue wildebeest), *Damaliscus* (blesbok/bontebok, tsessebe), *Hippotragus* (roan, sable), *Kobus* (puku, southern lechwe, waterbuck), *Madoqua* (Damara dik-dik), *Neotragus* (suni), *Oreotragus* (klipspringer), *Oryx* (gemsbok), *Ourebia* (oribi), *Pelea* (grey rhebok), *Philantomba* (blue duiker), *Raphicerus* (grysbok, Sharpe's grysbok, steenbok), *Redunca* (southern mountain reedbuck, southern reedbuck), *Sylvicapra* (common duiker), *Syncerus* (African buffalo), *Tragelaphus* (bushbuck, eland, kudu, nyala, sitatunga)

Zebras

Family: Equidae
Genus: *Equus* (Cape mountain zebra, Hartmann's mountain zebra, plains zebra)

Dogs, foxes, jackals and hyaenas

Family: Canidae
Genera: *Canis* (black-backed jackal, side-striped jackal), *Lycaon* (wild dog), *Otocyon* (bat-eared fox), *Vulpes* (Cape fox),

Family: Hyaenidae
Genera: *Crocuta* (spotted hyaena), *Hyaena* (brown hyaena), *Proteles* (aardwolf)

Cats

Family: Felidae
Genera: *Acinonyx* (cheetah), *Caracal* (caracal), *Felis* (black-footed cat, southern African wildcat), *Leptailurus* (serval), *Panthera* (leopard, lion)

Genets and civets

Family: Viverridae
Genera: *Civettictis* (African civet), *Genetta* (large-spotted genet, small-spotted genet)

Family: Nandiniidae
Genus: *Nandinia* (tree civet)

Pigs and hogs

Family: Suidae
Genera: *Phacochoerus* (common warthog), *Potamochoerus* (bushpig)

Dassies (hyraxes)

Family: Procaviidae
Genera: *Dendrohyrax* (tree dassie), *Heterohyrax* (yellow-spotted dassie), *Procavia* (Kaokoveld rock dassie, rock dassie)

Rabbits and hares

Family: Leporidae
Genera: *Lepus* (Cape hare, scrub hare), *Pronolagus* (Hewitt's red rock rabbit, Jameson's red rock rabbit, Natal red rock rabbit, Smith's red rock rabbit)

Family: Pedetidae
Genus: *Pedetes* (springhare)

Squirrels

Family: Sciuridae
Genera: *Funisciurus* (striped tree squirrel), *Heliosciurus* (mutable sun squirrel), *Paraxerus* (red bush squirrel, tree squirrel), *Sciurus* (grey squirrel), *Xerus* (Damara ground squirrel, South African ground squirrel)

Mongooses and suricate

Family: Herpestidae
Genera: *Atilax* (water mongoose), *Bdeogale* (bushy-tailed mongoose), *Cynictis* (yellow mongoose), *Galerella* (Cape grey mongoose, slender mongoose), *Helogale* (dwarf mongoose), *Herpestes* (large grey mongoose), *Ichneumia* (white-tailed mongoose), *Mungos* (banded mongoose), *Paracynictis* (Selous' mongoose), *Rhynchogale* (Meller's mongoose), *Suricata* (suricate)

Otters

Family: Mustelidae
Genera: *Aonyx* (Cape clawless otter), *Lutra* (spotted-necked otter)

Badger, polecat and weasel

Family: Mustelidae
Genera: *Ictonyx* (striped polecat), *Mellivora* (honey badger), *Poecilogale* (African striped weasel)

Primates

Family: Cercopithecidae
Genera: *Papio* (chacma baboon), *Cercopithecus* (Sykes' monkey, vervet monkey)

Family: Galagidae
Genera: *Galago* (lesser bushbaby), *Galagoides* (Grant's lesser bushbaby), *Otolemur* (thick-tailed bushbaby)

Honey badger

Further reading and references

De Graaff, G. 1992. *Animals of the Kruger National Park*, 2nd ed. Struik, Cape Town.

Frandsen, R. 2004. *Southern Africa's Mammals: A Field Guide*. Honeyguide Publications, Johannesburg.

Pienaar, U de V., Joubert, SCJ, Hall-Martin, A, de Graff, G and Rautenbach, IL. 1987. *Field Guide to the Mammals of the Kruger National Park*. Struik, Cape Town

Smithers, RHN. 2000. *Smithers' Mammals of Southern Africa: A Field Guide*. Struik, Cape Town.

Stuart, C and T. 2006. *Field Guide to the Larger Mammals of Southern Africa*. Struik, Cape Town.

Stuart, C and T. 2007. *Field Guide to Mammals of Southern Africa*, 4th ed. Struik, Cape Town.

Walker, C. 1988. *Signs of the Wild*. Struik, Cape Town.

Zaloumis, EA and Cross, R. 1974. *A Field Guide to the Antelope of Southern Africa*. Natal Branch of the Wildlife Society of Southern Africa, Durban.

Index to scientific names

Index to Afrikaans common names

Index to English common names